Leckie × Leckie

Scotland's leading educational publishers

CW00687199

Higher
HUMAN BIOLOGY
SUCCESS GUIDE

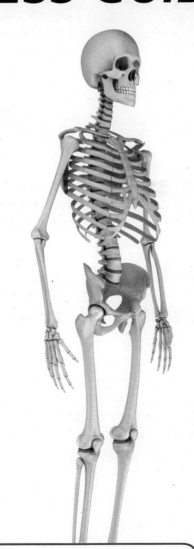

Higher HUMAN BIOLOGY SUCCESS GUIDE

John Di Mambro • Stuart White

© 2017 Leckie & Leckie Ltd

001/12042017

10 9 8 7 6 5 4 3 2 1

All rights reserved. No part of this publication may be reproduced, stored in a retrieval system, or transmitted in any form or by any means, electronic, mechanical, photocopying, recording or otherwise, without the prior written permission of the Publisher or a licence permitting restricted copying in the United Kingdom issued by the Copyright Licensing Agency Ltd., 90 Tottenham Court Road, London W1T 4LP.

ISBN 9780008209025

Published by
Leckie & Leckie Ltd
An imprint of HarperCollins*Publishers*
Westerhill Road, Bishopbriggs, Glasgow, G64 2QT
T: 0844 576 8126   F: 0844 576 8131
leckieandleckie@harpercollins.co.uk   www.leckieandleckie.co.uk

Commissioning editor: Clare Souza
Managing editor: Craig Balfour

Special thanks to
Dylan Hamilton (copyedit)
Jess White (proofread)
Louise Robb (proofread)
Lauren Reid (editorial)
Lisa Footit (index)
QBS (layout and illustration)
Ink Tank (cover design)

A CIP Catalogue record for this book is available from the British Library.

Acknowledgements
Fig 2.26 Public Domain; Fig 2.645 © nathan Benn / Getty images; Fig 3.48 JASPERIMAGE / Shutterstock.com; Fig 3.49 © 1000 Words / Shutterstock.com; Fig 3.51 © FRANCK FIFE / Getty Images; Fig 4.18 (top) © Davide Calabresi / Shutterstock.com

Whilst every effort has been made to trace the copyright holders, in cases where this has been unsuccessful, or if any have inadvertently been overlooked, the Publishers would gladly receive any information enabling them to rectify any error or omission at the first opportunity.

Printed in Italy by Grafica Veneta Spa

MIX
Paper from
responsible sources
FSC www.fsc.org   FSC™ C007454

FSC™ is a non-profit international organisation established to promote the responsible management of the world's forests. Products carrying the FSC label are independently certified to assure consumers that they come from forests that are managed to meet the social, economic and ecological needs of present and future generations, and other controlled sources.

Find out more about HarperCollins and the environment at
www.harpercollins.co.uk/green

Unit 1: Human Cells

Contents

Unit 2: Physiology and Health

Unit 3: Neurobiology and Communication

Contents

Unit 4: Immunology and Public Health

Introduction

The CfE Higher

The CfE Higher Human Biology course aims to develop your interest and enthusiasm for biology as it applies to human beings, as well as developing the skills required to function as a scientist in a modern-day context. The course is wide-ranging and draws on a number of different scientific disciplines involving cellular processes, physiological mechanisms, how humans communicate and the biology of how human populations interact. The skills developed will allow you to adapt to new situations, solve problems, make decisions based on evidence and evaluate how current developments in science might impact on your own health.

Structure

The CfE Higher Human Biology course is made up of four units:

- Human Cells (eight topics)
- Physiology and Health (eight topics)
- Neurobiology and Communication (four topics)
- Immunology and Public Health (four topics).

Course assessment

The final grade you obtain in Higher Human Biology will depend on how well you pass the final national examination (worth 100 marks), which tests all four units, as well as passing the course assessments. The course assessments take place where you are currently studying and each one results in a pass or a fail, not a grade. There is an example of each type of course assessment at the end of each of the four units in this Success Guide. Linked to the course is an assignment (worth 20 marks), which is related to a topic of your choice associated with one of the four units. This is not an examination but an open-book exercise completed under close supervision during which you will write an account of the research you have done on your selected topic. The assignment is not assessed by your current teacher but is sent to SQA for marking.

A fuller explanation of the aims and assessment strategies for the course can be found on the SQA website at www.sqa.org.uk.

How to use this book

This Success Guide focuses on the final examination, which requires an in-depth knowledge of the course content to achieve a good grade. It is a revision aid which will also help you as the course continues. The guide follows the unit structure of the course as detailed in the SQA guidelines to help you learn in a logical and user-friendly way.

Each unit ends with an assessment giving you an opportunity to review how well you know the unit content, and to practise for the SQA course assessments, which must be passed. Answers to the unit assessments can be found at the back of the book.

Many assessment questions test your knowledge of the meaning of a particular word or phrase. To help you learn words and meanings, a glossary of terms has been included at the back of this book. One revision strategy you may consider is creating flashcards of these glossary terms and there are several free online programs which will help you make flashcards.

Division and differentiation in human cells

Cellular differentiation

TOP TIP

Differentiated cells have a specific function and are unable to become any other type of cell.

Somatic cells divide by **mitosis** to form more somatic cells. **Cellular differentiation** is the process where a cell changes from one cell type to another cell type. A cell becomes a more specialised type of cell through **gene expression**. It develops more specialised functions by **expressing** the **genes** characteristic for that type of cell. For example, a **stem cell** can **differentiate** into a skin cell by switching on those genes which code for particular proteins, and by switching off the others which don't.

Stem cells

Stem cells are **unspecialised somatic cells** in animals that can divide to make copies of themselves (self-renew) and/or differentiate into **specialised** cells. They become specialised after differentiation when specific genes are expressed ('switched on') while others are not ('switched off'). This helps a wide variety of cells within animals to be differentiated from unspecialised stem cells, as shown in **Figure 1.1**.

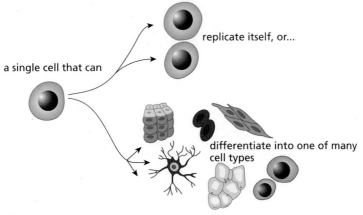

a single cell that can

replicate itself, or...

differentiate into one of many cell types

Figure 1.1: *Functions of stem cells*

Tissue stem cells

Tissue stem cells are involved in the growth, repair and renewal of the cells found in that tissue. For example, they replenish differentiated cells that need to be replaced. They are **multipotent** and capable of developing into a more limited range of cell types. For example, the blood stem cells found in red bone marrow produce the various blood cell types.

> ### TOP TIP
> Skin, blood and nerve cells can all be derived from tissue stem cells. These can be used therapeutically in corneal transplants and bone marrow transplants.

Embryonic stem cells

The cells in **embryos** are **pluripotent** and can make all of the differentiated cell types of the body. When grown in a laboratory by scientists these cells are called **embryonic stem cells**. These cells can self-renew under appropriate laboratory conditions. They can be used **therapeutically** as a source of stem cells in research and medical therapy, as shown in **Figure 1.2**.

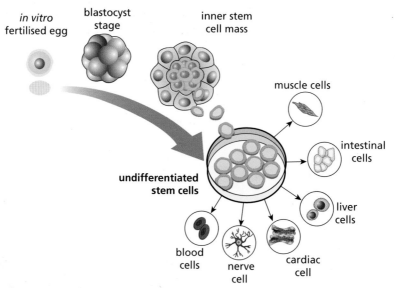

Figure 1.2: *Embryonic stem cell isolation and culture*

> ### TOP TIP
> The main body tissue types are epithelial, connective, muscle and nerve. The body's organs are formed from a variety of these tissues.

Germline cells

Germline cells divide by mitosis to produce more germline cells or by **meiosis** to produce **haploid gametes**. **Mutations** in germline cells are passed to offspring. Mutations in somatic cells are not passed to offspring.

Research and therapeutic uses of stem cells

Research and therapeutic uses of stem cells include:

- stem cells are used therapeutically in the repair of damaged or diseased organs or tissues, for example, in corneal transplants or as skin grafts for burns
- stem cell research provides information on how cell processes such as cell growth, differentiation and gene regulation function
- stem cells are used as model cells to observe how diseases develop
- stem cells are used in **drug testing** of potential medications.

The ethical issues of stem cell use and the regulation of their use

The use of embryonic stem cells raises **ethical issues**. These include:

- regulating the use of embryo stem cells
- the use of **induced pluripotent stem cells**
- the use of **nuclear transfer techniques**.

Regulations ensure that the use of stem cells in research and therapy is carried out in accordance with UK law. This guarantees that procedures regarding the procurement of stem cells are conducted safely.

Cancer cells

Cancer cells divide excessively and produce a mass of abnormal cells called a **tumour**. They do not respond to regulatory signals and may fail to attach to one another. When cancer cells fail to attach to each other they spread through the body to form **secondary tumours**.

Structure and replication of DNA

Structure of DNA

Deoxyribonucleic acid or DNA is the substance that makes up the genetic material in cells and gives the cell its **genotype**.

DNA is composed of very long molecules made up of repeating chemical units called **nucleotides**.

A nucleotide has three chemical parts:

- an organic base
- a phosphate group
- a central deoxyribose sugar.

There are four different organic bases:

- adenine (A)
- guanine (G)
- thymine (T)
- cytosine (C).

Nucleotides are linked together to make a long strand of DNA. This arrangement produces a sugar-phosphate backbone with the bases attached, as shown in **Figure 1.3**. The 5′ end has a phosphate attached to the fifth carbon of the deoxyribose sugar. The 3′ end has the third carbon of the deoxyribose sugar exposed.

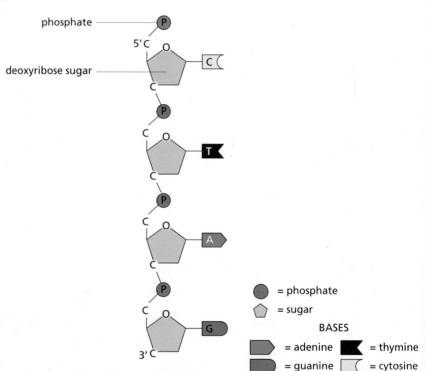

Figure 1.3: *Short strand of DNA with four nucleotides on a 3′ to 5′ sugar phosphate backbone*

Two strands are joined together through **weak hydrogen bonds** that link **complementary** pairs of nucleotide bases.

Adenine always pairs with thymine. Guanine always pairs with cytosine.

The strands run in opposite directions from carbon 3′ at one end to carbon 5′ at the other end, but in opposite directions and are described as **antiparallel**, as shown in **Figure 1.4**.

The molecule is wound into a double-stranded helix, as shown in **Figure 1.5**.

Chromosomes consist of tightly coiled DNA and are packaged with associated proteins, as shown in **Figure 1.6**.

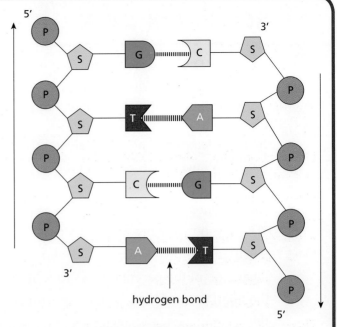

Figure 1.4: *Antiparallel strands of DNA*

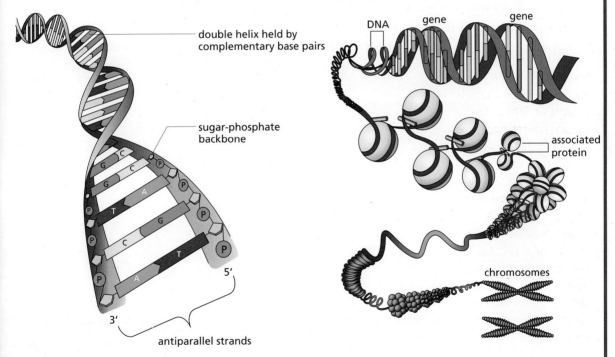

Figure 1.5: *Double helix of DNA showing antiparallel sugar-phosphate backbones joined by complementary base pairs*

Figure 1.6: *Chromosome showing associated proteins*

Replication of DNA

It is essential that DNA is able to replicate (make more exact copies of itself) so that all cells have enough genetic information to be able to divide by mitosis.

In order for DNA replication to occur, certain substances must be present within the nucleus:

- the DNA template (the parental strands allow an exact copy to be made)
- free DNA nucleotide bases (all four types)
- enzymes (such as **DNA polymerase** and **ligase**)
- **primers** (their presence is required to begin replication)
- **ATP** (to supply energy for the process).

DNA replication is shown in **Figure 1.7** and involves the following stages:

1. Separation of the parental DNA to form two templates.
2. The free DNA nucleotides pairing with complementary bases on template strands.
3. The sugar-phosphate backbones forming on new strands.
4. Two daughter DNA molecules forming (both of which are genetically identical to the parental DNA).

During the first stage the original parental DNA is separated using an enzyme and ATP to break the weak hydrogen bonds between base pairs. The strands then unwind and unzip to form two template strands. This occurs at several points along the DNA molecule.

In the second stage a primer is attached to the 3′ end of the parental DNA strand. An enzyme called DNA polymerase begins to join free DNA nucleotides to the template strands.

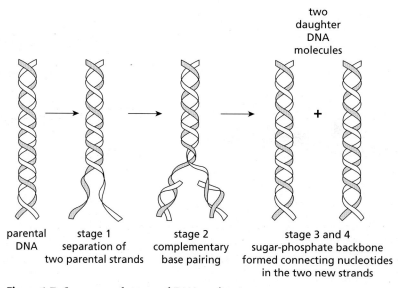

Figure 1.7: *Summary of stages of DNA replication*

Leading strand

On the leading strand, nucleotides are added from the deoxyribose (3′) end of the parental strand in one direction in a continuous fashion.

Lagging strand

The lagging strand is antiparallel to the leading strand but replication cannot begin at the 5′ end. Instead it is replicated in fragments, starting with primer at the 3′ end. Nucleotides are added in a discontinuous fashion as more primer is added to the lagging strand, as shown in **Figure 1.8**.

The third stage involves the use of the enzyme ligase, which joins together the small fragments of newly formed DNA in the lagging strand to form a sugar-phosphate backbone. The daughter DNA molecules are formed in the fourth stage.

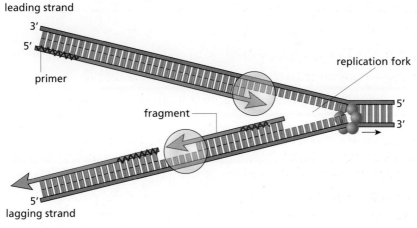

Figure 1.8: *Leading and lagging strand replication*

TOP TIP

To produce new cells and pass on the correct genetic instructions to new generations, DNA replication must create identical copies of the information contained in the DNA.

TOP TIP

The exact replication of sequences of the bases makes one species distinct from another.

Gene expression

Gene expression **(Figure 1.9)** is controlled by the regulation of **transcription** and **translation**. The genetic code processed by transcription and translation is found in all forms of life.

An organism's **phenotype** is determined by the proteins produced as a result of gene expression. This is influenced by **intracellular** and extracellular environmental factors. An organism's DNA sequences are called its genome. Not all the genes are expressed in every cell in an organism.

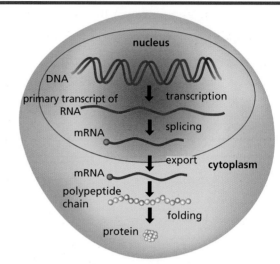

Figure 1.9: *Overview of gene expression*

Ribonucleic acid (RNA)

RNA is vital to the process of protein synthesis. It has some similarities to DNA but differs in three ways:

1. RNA is a single-stranded molecule (DNA is double-stranded).

2. RNA has the same bases as DNA except for uracil, which replaces thymine.

3. RNA has a ribose sugar (in contrast to DNA's deoxyribose sugar), as shown in **Figure 1.10**.

Feature	DNA	RNA
number of strands	2	1
bases	A T G C	A U G C
sugar	deoxyribose	ribose

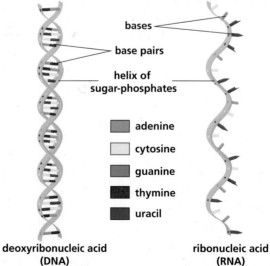

bases

base pairs

helix of sugar-phosphates

- adenine
- cytosine
- guanine
- thymine
- uracil

deoxyribonucleic acid (DNA)

ribonucleic acid (RNA)

Figure 1.10: *DNA and RNA*

The main forms of RNA are:

1. Messenger RNA (mRNA) carries a copy of the DNA code from the nucleus to the ribosome). It has a linear form and groups of three bases known as **codons**.

2. Ribosomal RNA (rRNA), which, along with ribosomal protein, forms protein-synthesising organelles called **ribosomes**.

3. Transfer RNA (tRNA), molecules each carry a specific amino acid and are involved in the second part of protein synthesis. They have a folded shape and an **anticodon**, each of which attaches to a different amino acid at an attachment site.

The three types of RNA are shown in **Figure 1.11**.

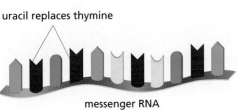

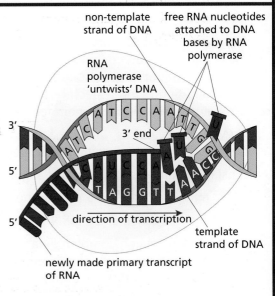

Figure 1.11: *Types of RNA*

Protein synthesis

Protein synthesis is a process in which instructions from DNA sequences are carried to ribosomes and proteins are synthesised.

Transcription

Transcription, shown in **Figure 1.12**, is the first phase of gene expression. The particular DNA sequence for the gene to be expressed is copied onto a primary transcript of mRNA in the following process:

1. **RNA polymerase** moves along the DNA and unwinds the double helix.

2. Hydrogen bonds between the base pairs break, unzipping the double helix.

3. As RNA polymerase breaks the bonds, it synthesises a primary transcript of mRNA on the DNA template strand using free RNA nucleotides. These RNA nucleotides form hydrogen bonds with the exposed DNA bases by complementary base pairing.

4. A primary RNA transcript is formed.

Figure 1.12: *Transcription*

Splicing

The primary transcript is made of **introns** and **exons**.

5. The introns of the primary transcript of mRNA are **non-coding** and are removed.

6. The exons are **coding** regions and are joined together to form mature transcript.

7. This process is called **RNA splicing**.

This process is summarised in **Figure 1.13**.

After leaving the nucleus through a pore in the nuclear membrane, the mature transcript travels through the cytoplasm to a ribosome for the next stage of protein synthesis.

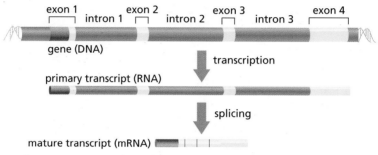

Figure 1.13: *RNA splicing from primary to mature transcript*

Translation

The mature transcript of mRNA arrives and attaches itself to a site on the ribosome. The sequence of codons on the mRNA is read as the complementary tRNA anticodons carrying the appropriate amino acids are brought to the ribosome.

As the mRNA strand moves along the ribosome it continues to be read and amino acids continue to bind together using **peptide bonds**. As the chain grows, the sequence of amino acids becomes a **polypeptide**. tRNA then exits from the ribosome.

The starting and end points of the chain formed are determined by triplets of mRNA called start and **stop codons**, respectively. The mRNA codon AUG, which codes for the amino acid methionine, also acts as a **start codon**. The mRNA codons UAA, UGA and UAG do not code for a specific amino acid. Instead they act as stop codons, which terminate the polypeptide chain formation.

tRNA can carry out its function as it folds forming a triplet anticodon site and an attachment site for a specific amino acid.

Translation can be summarised in **Figure 1.14** and the following stages:

1. mRNA attaches to a site on the ribosome.

2. The first codon of the mRNA is called a start codon and this starts the translation process.

3. Codons match complementary bases on the anticodon of tRNA, which transports appropriate amino acids to the ribosome. The anticodon on a tRNA molecule is specific to only one amino acid.

4. The amino acids form a chain, joined together by peptide bonds.

5. This chain is called a polypeptide.

6. The last codon of the mRNA is called a stop codon and this stops the translation process.

7. The polypeptide leaves the ribosome once completed.

8. The way in which polypeptide chains are assembled determines the structure and function of the finished protein.

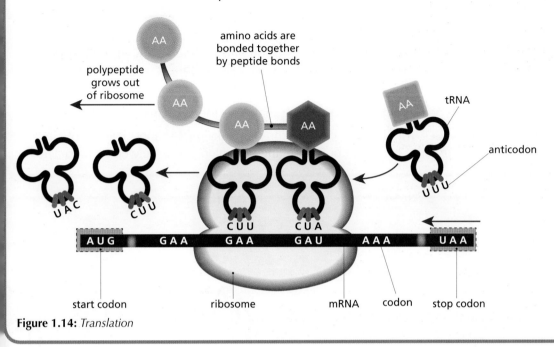

Figure 1.14: *Translation*

Proteins

Different proteins can be expressed from one gene. This is a result of alternative RNA splicing and **post-translational modification**.

Different mRNA molecules are produced from the same primary transcript.

After translation, some proteins need further modification to enable them to perform their functions.

Post-translational protein structure modification can be achieved in different ways:

- by cutting and combining polypeptide chains
- by adding phosphate or carbohydrate groups to the protein, shown in **Figure 1.15**.

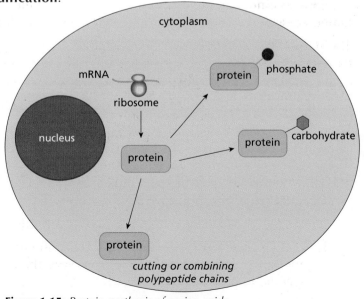

Figure 1.15: *Protein synthesis of amino acids*

Genes and proteins in health and disease

Protein structure

Proteins produced after translation and modification have a variety of structures and functions. The polypeptide chains, composed of amino acids joined by peptide bonds, are sequenced in an order which is specific to the protein function. They are shaped in a way dependent on their amino acid sequence.

There are 20 different types of amino acids which make up the proteins.

Protein shape variation arises from folding, creating three-dimensional shapes. Folding of polypeptide chains is caused by hydrogen bonds linking and interactions between amino acids.

Mutations

Mutations are random changes in the genome (**Figure 1.16**) that can result in either no protein or an altered protein being expressed. These range from a change in a single base to changes in chromosome structure or number. If the change to the genome results in an alteration to the organism's phenotype, it is called a mutant organism.

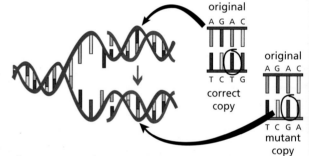

Figure 1.16: *A change in the genome*

Mutations are random and spontaneous. The frequency of mutations can be increased by exposure to **mutagenic agents**. Mutations can occur during DNA replication or gamete formation. Mutations cause alterations to the genome which may contribute to the evolution of a species.

Single gene mutations

A single nucleotide base change results in single gene mutations. The DNA nucleotide sequence is altered by the **substitution**, **insertion** or **deletion** of nucleotides. The impact on the protein synthesised can be either minor or major, depending on the type of mutation. The table below shows single gene mutations and these are illustrated in **Figure 1.17**.

Single gene mutation	DNA base sequence	Impact of gene mutation
none	ATG CGT CGA	
substitution	ATG CCT CGA	minor change to protein structure
insertion	ATG CGG TCG	major change to protein structure
deletion	ATG CTC GA	major change to protein structure

If a single nucleotide is substituted then this will only change one codon, resulting in a minor change to the protein produced. Single nucleotide substitutions include **missense**, **nonsense** and **splice site** mutations.

Substitution	Change	End effect on protein produced
missense	one codon to another	different amino acid translated
		possible change in protein shape
		may have no effect
nonsense	a codon to a stop codon	shortens the protein
		may become non-functional or its function will be changed
splice site	change in nucleotide at a splice site (between intron and exon)	may prevent splicing
		this results in a very different protein being synthesised because introns may be left in the primary transcript

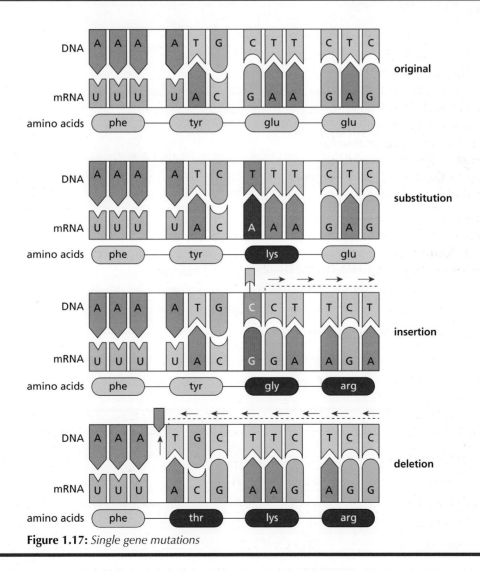

Figure 1.17: *Single gene mutations*

Nucleotide insertions or deletions result in **frameshift mutations** or an expansion of a nucleotide sequence repeat. When the codon is translated at the ribosome into an amino acid, that amino acid and all the subsequent ones are changed. This may result in a faulty, non-functional or alternative protein. Mutations in some non-coding DNA sequences can result in changes to the way certain genes are expressed. The **frameshift** effects of insertion and deletion are illustrated in **Figure 1.18**.

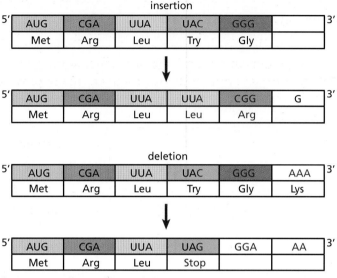

Figure 1.18: *Effects of frameshift mutations on amino acid sequences*

Nucleotide sequence repeats

Nucleotide sequence repeats are short DNA sequences that are repeated a number of times. For example, a trinucleotide repeat is made up of three base pair sequences. A tetranucleotide repeat is made up of four base pair sequences. The expansion of a nucleotide sequence repeat increases by the number of times that the short DNA sequence is repeated. This type of mutation can cause the resulting protein to function differently or not at all.

Chromosome structure mutations

Chromosome structure mutations are those which affect whole chromosomes or sections of the genome. They are alterations to the structure of one or more chromosomes. They include:

- **duplication**
- **deletion**
- **translocation**.

Each of the mutations is described in the table below and in **Figure 1.19**.

Mutation	Description
duplication	produced when extra copies of genes are generated on a chromosome
deletion	results from the breakage of a chromosome in two places in which the genetic material becomes lost during cell division
translocation	the piece of chromosome detaches from one chromosome and moves to a new position on another chromosome

The mutated chromosome segments are often large and affect many genes. This results in large alterations in the genome and the proteins produced, many of which will be defective. Substantial changes in chromosome mutations can make them lethal.

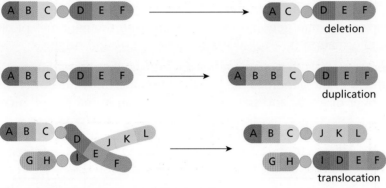

Figure 1.19: *Chromosome structure mutations*

Human genomics

Sequencing DNA

TOP TIP

The Human Genome Project, which was finished in 2003, sequenced three billion nucleotide bases and found around 20,000 genes in the human genome.

Genomic sequencing is a process in which the order of the nucleotide bases along an organism's genome is determined.

The sequence of nucleotide bases can be determined for individual genes and for entire genomes. This helps identify genes and genome sequences that are responsible for particular diseases and conditions, and helps identify genomic mutations and variations.

Bioinformatics is used to compare sequence data. This enables complete genomes to be sequenced very quickly.

Systematics compares human genome sequence data and the genomes of other species in order to provide information on evolutionary relationships and origins.

Comparing genomes reveals that many genes are conserved across different organisms. There are similarities in the genomes of species which are outwardly very different. For example, the number of genes and size of the genomes in humans and mice is similar.

Comparison of genome sizes of different organisms			
Organism	Chromosome number	Estimated size (base pairs)	Estimated gene number
human	46	3 billion	25,000
mouse	40	2.9 billion	25,000
fruit fly	8	165 million	13,000
plant	10	157 million	25,000
roundworm	12	97 million	19,000
yeast	32	12 million	6,000
bacteria	1	4.6 million	3,200

Personalised medicine

The human genome was sequenced in 2003, at a cost of £3 billion. Due to advances in technology, an individual human genome can now be sequenced cheaply and quickly, for a fraction of that cost, and in days rather than years. Therefore, obtaining an individual's personal genome is relatively easy and this information could be used in a number of ways in the future.

One way in which this data could be used is to identify mutations within the genome. As discussed before, these can either be harmful (the changes result in wrong/no protein forming) or neutral (the change has no negative effect).

Analysis of an individual's genome leads to **personalised medicine**. Using **pharmacogenetics** the success of a particular treatment can be predicted. The identification of the genomic change responsible for a genetic disorder enables a specific treatment to be applied. Individual treatments are personalised, as shown in **Figure 1.20**, and more likely to succeed.

Several diseases and conditions are the result of a combination of genetic and environmental factors. This causes difficulties when it comes to treatment. These diseases can be complex and can be caused by other organisms, such as viruses.

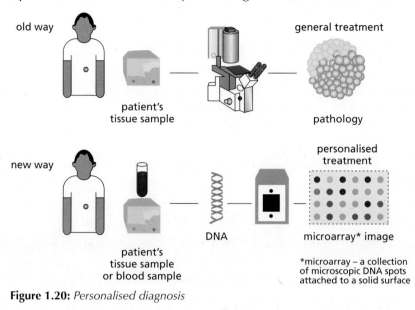

Figure 1.20: *Personalised diagnosis*

Amplification and detection of DNA sequences

The **polymerase chain reaction** (PCR) is a technique for the **amplification** of DNA *in vitro*.

In PCR the primers are chosen to target specific sequences at the two ends of the region of DNA being amplified. This involves the use of a **thermal cycler**.

Similar to DNA replication, PCR has some initial requirements for the process to occur. These are:

- DNA template
- free DNA nucleotides (all four types)
- heat-tolerant DNA polymerase (enzyme)
- primers – artificially made, short, single strands of DNA that use bases complementary to those at either end of the DNA fragment to be copied.

Figure 1.21 shows the general stages of the PCR cycle.

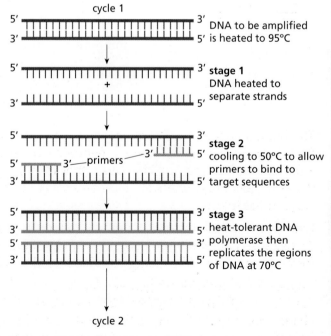

Figure 1.21: *The three stages of PCR*

1. DNA heated to 95°C to separate strands, then cooled to 50°C to for primer binding.

2. Cooling allows primers to bind to target sequences.

3. Heat-tolerant DNA polymerase then replicates the region of DNA at 70°C.

4. Repeated cycles of heating and cooling amplify this region of DNA as shown in **Figure 1.22**.

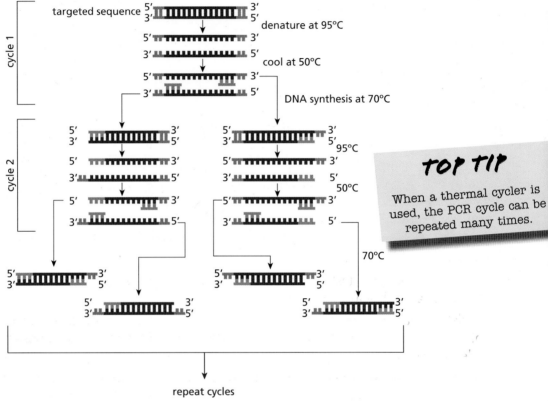

Figure 1.22: *Repeated cycles of PCR amplifying the original DNA strand*

TOP TIP

When a thermal cycler is used, the PCR cycle can be repeated many times.

Figure 1.23 shows the stages and temperatures.

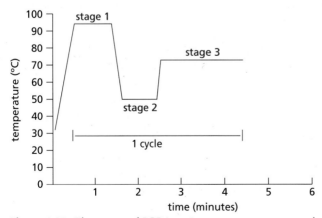

Figure 1.23: *The stages of PCR in a time vs temperature graph*

TOP TIP

DNA profiling can also be called DNA fingerprinting, DNA testing or DNA typing.

When a thermal cycler is used, the PCR cycle can be repeated many times, as shown in **Figure 1.24**. **Arrays** of **DNA probes** are used to detect the presence of specific sequences in samples of DNA. The probes are short, single-stranded fragments of DNA that are complementary to a specific sequence. **Fluorescent labelling** enables detection.

DNA profiling is a forensic technique used to identify individuals by characteristics of their DNA.

Applications of DNA profiling enable the identification of individuals through comparison of regions of the genome with highly variable numbers of repetitive sequences of DNA.

Practical applications of PCR

The DNA amplified by PCR can be used in many ways, such as:

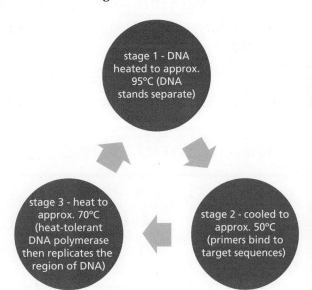

Figure 1.24: *Repeated cycles of heating and cooling amplify the region of DNA*

- DNA sequencing (creating many copies of a small piece of DNA so it can be fully sequenced)

- genetic-mapping studies (for example, the Human Genome Project)

- forensic and parental testing (critical in forensic analysis when only a trace amount of DNA is available as evidence)

- sex determination in prenatal cells (sex can be determined by the presence of a unique sequence on the Y chromosome (SRY gene)). If the SRY gene is present it is male, if it is absent it is female

- classification of species into taxonomic groups based on DNA sequences (small fragments of DNA can be amplified to enable genomes to be compared)

- screening for, and diagnosis of, genetic disorders, for example, cystic fibrosis and Huntington's disease.

Metabolic pathways

Cell metabolism

Cell metabolism is the collective term for the thousands of biochemical reactions that occur within a living cell. A metabolic pathway is a series of chemical reactions occurring within a cell. Metabolism encompasses the integrated and controlled pathways of enzyme-catalysed reactions within a cell.

Anabolic and catabolic pathways

Anabolism

Anabolic pathways require energy and involve **biosynthetic processes**, shown in **Figure 1.25**.

Catabolism

Catabolic pathways release energy and involve the breakdown of molecules, shown in **Figure 1.26**.

These pathways can have reversible and irreversible stages and alternative routes. Metabolic pathways may exist that can bypass stages in a pathway, shown in **Figure 1.27**.

An example of a linked pathway can be seen in **Figure 1.28**.

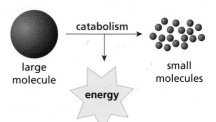

Figure 1.25: *A simple anabolic pathway*

Figure 1.26: *A simple catabolic pathway*

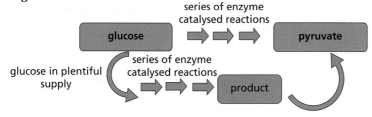

Figure 1.27: *Bypass pathway when glucose is in plentiful supply*

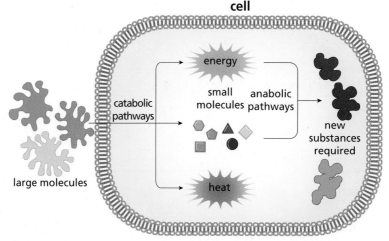

Figure 1.28: *How catabolic and anabolic reactions can be linked*

Control of metabolic pathways

Metabolic pathways can be controlled in a number of ways, for example, through the presence or absence of particular enzymes regulating the rate of reaction of key enzymes within the pathway.

The pathways can also be regulated by controlling **intracellular** and **extracellular** molecules.

Induced fit

Induced fit describes the change when a molecule of **substrate** enters the **active site**. The enzyme molecule and the active site change shape making the active site fit very closely round the substrate molecule. This is shown in **Figure 1.29**.

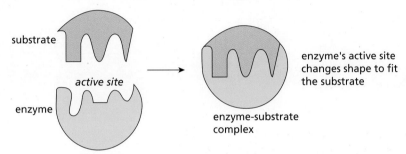

Figure 1.29: *Induced fit of enzyme's active site interacting with specific substrate*

The active site is not a rigid structure. It is flexible and dynamic. The enzyme is specific to its substrate. It will only bind to one particular substrate because the shape of the active site has to match the shape of the substrate.

The substrate has a high **affinity** for the active site.

Activation energy is needed to break chemical bonds in the reactant chemicals. Induced fit lowers the activation energy needed by reactants and increases the reaction rate.

Multi-enzyme complexes

Enzymes often act in groups or as **multi-enzyme complexes**. An example is shown in **Figure 1.30**.

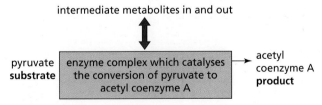

Figure 1.30: *Pyruvate dehydrogenase multi-enzyme complex*

TOP TIP

The majority of metabolic reactions are reversible and the presence of a substrate or the removal of a product will drive a sequence of reactions in a particular direction.

Control of metabolic pathways

Control of metabolic pathways is achieved through competitive, **non-competitive** and **feedback inhibition** of enzymes.

- Molecules of a **competitive inhibitor** compete with molecules of the substrate for the active sites on the enzyme, as shown in **Figure 1.31**. The inhibitor is able to do this because its molecular structure is similar to that of the substrate and it can attach itself to the enzyme's active site. Competitive inhibition can be reversed by increasing substrate concentration. This is shown in **Figure 1.32**.

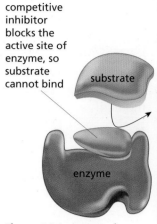

competitive inhibitor blocks the active site of enzyme, so substrate cannot bind

substrate

enzyme

Figure 1.31: *Action of a non-competitor inhibitor*

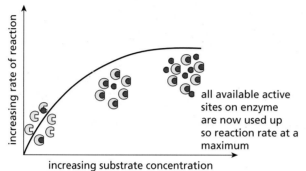

all available active sites on enzyme are now used up so reaction rate at a maximum

increasing rate of reaction

increasing substrate concentration

Figure 1.32: *Effect of increasing substrate concentration on the rate of reaction*

- A non-competitive inhibitor does not combine directly with an enzyme's active site. Instead it becomes attached to a non-active site and changes the shape of the enzyme molecule. This is shown in **Figure 1.33**.

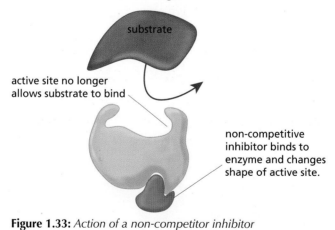

substrate

active site no longer allows substrate to bind

non-competitive inhibitor binds to enzyme and changes shape of active site.

Figure 1.33: *Action of a non-competitor inhibitor*

- Control of metabolic pathways is also achieved through feedback inhibition of enzymes. The rate at which some metabolic pathways progress is controlled by a build-up of the end product. In feedback inhibition, the end product binds to one enzyme in the metabolic pathway. This alters the shape of this enzyme's active site and stops the pathway shown in **Figure 1.34**. This prevents too much end product from being produced. As the concentration of the end product drops, inhibition ceases and the pathway resumes again. This is shown in **Figure 1.35**.

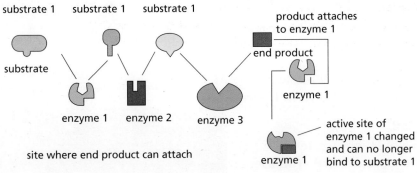

Figure 1.34: *Action of end product causing change in shape of the active site of enzyme 1*

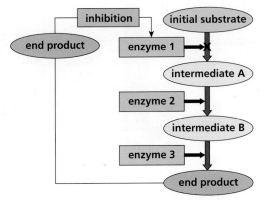

Figure 1.35: *End product inhibition of a metabolic pathway*

Cellular respiration

ATP

ATP is used to transfer energy to synthetic pathways and other cellular processes where energy is required.

Phosphorylation is an enzyme-controlled process by which a phosphate group is added to a molecule. For example, phosphorylation occurs when P_i combines with low-energy ADP to form high-energy ATP shown in **Figure 1.36**.

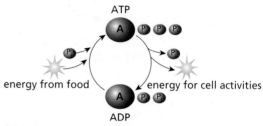

Figure 1.36: *Transfer of energy from ATP breakdown*

ATP-synthase

The return flow of **H ions** rotates part of the membrane protein **ATP synthase**, catalysing the synthesis of ATP. This is shown in **Figure 1.37**.

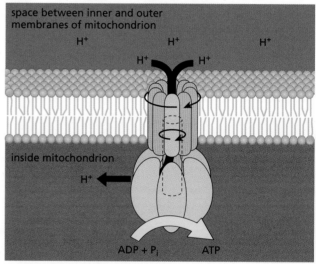

Figure 1.37: *Action of ATP synthase*

Metabolic pathways of cellular respiration

There are three stages in cellular respiration:

- **glycolysis** (takes place in cytoplasm)
- **citric acid cycle** (takes place in the **matrix of the mitochondria**)
- **electron transport** chain (takes place in the inner membrane of mitochondria or cristae).

During this process, glucose is broken down, and hydrogen ions and electrons are removed by **dehydrogenase enzymes**, releasing ATP.

Glycolysis

Glycolysis takes place in the cytoplasm. Glycolysis is the breakdown of glucose (6C) to **pyruvate** (3C).

The phosphorylation of intermediates in glycolysis in an **energy investment stage** leads to the generation of more ATP in an **energy pay-off stage** giving a **net gain** of ATP.

To start the process energy from two ATP molecules is required. The series of reactions eventually produces four ATP molecules resulting in a net gain of two ATPs from glycolysis. This is shown in **Figure 1.38**.

Hydrogen ions released at this stage are transported by NAD to the electron transport chain.

In the absence of oxygen, pyruvate undergoes **fermentation** to **lactate** or ethanol and carbon dioxide. This is shown in **Figure 1.39**.

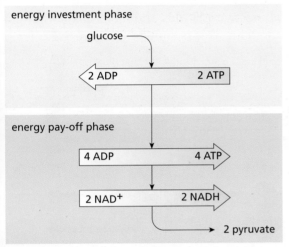

Figure 1.38: *The two phases of glycolysis*

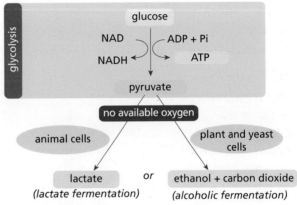

Figure 1.39: *Fermentation in the cytoplasm of animal, plant and yeast cells*

Citric acid cycle

This stage takes place in the matrix of the mitochondria. Pyruvate is broken down to an acetyl group that combines with coenzyme A then transferred to the citric acid cycle as **acetyl coenzyme A,** shown in **Figure 1.40**.

The acetyl coenzyme A combines with **oxaloacetate** to form **citrate**. The enzyme-mediated stages of the cycle follow resulting in the generation of ATP, the release of carbon dioxide, and the regeneration of oxaloacetate. This is summarised in **Figure 1.41**.

Dehydrogenase enzymes remove H ions and electrons, which are passed to **coenzymes NAD** or **FAD** (forming either NADH or FADH$_2$) in glycolysis and citric acid pathways. Two ATP are produced during the citric acid cycle.

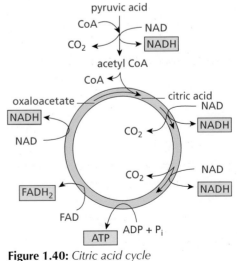

Figure 1.40: *Citric acid cycle*

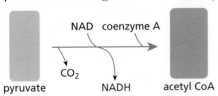

Figure 1.41: *Formation of acetyl coenzyme A from coenzyme A (CoA)*

Electron transport chain

This stage takes place on the folded inner membrane of the mitochondrial cristae. The electron transport chain is a collection of proteins attached to a membrane.

The H ions and high-energy electrons are passed to the electron transport chain resulting in the synthesis of ATP which involves high-energy. ATP synthesis involves high-energy electrons pumping H ions across a membrane. The return flow of these ions rotates part of the membrane protein ATP synthesis, catalysing the synthesis of ATP.

Oxygen is the final electron acceptor, which combines with H ions and electrons, forming water. Most ATP (32) are produced by the electron chain. This is shown in **Figure 1.42**.

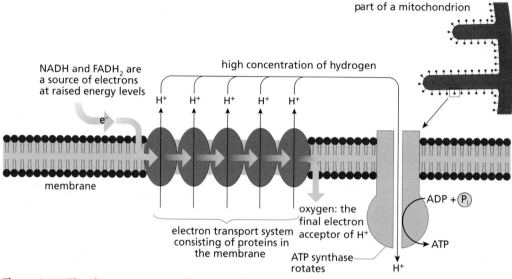

Figure 1.42: *The electron transport chain and ATP synthase*

Substrates for respiration

Starch and **glycogen** are broken down to glucose for use as **respiratory substrates**. Other molecules can be converted to glucose or intermediates of glycolysis for use as respiratory substrates. Proteins can be broken down to amino acids and converted to intermediates of glycolysis and the citric acid cycle for use as respiratory substrates. Fats can also be broken down to intermediates of glycolysis and the citric acid cycle. A summary is shown in **Figure 1.43**.

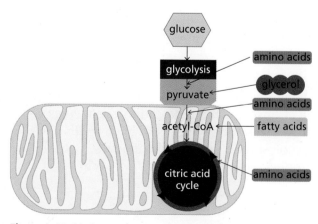

Figure 1.43: *Various substrates used in cell respiration and their points of entry*

Regulation of the pathways of cellular respiration by feedback inhibition

The cell conserves its resources by only producing ATP when required.

The supply of ATP increases as rates of glycolysis and the citric acid cycle increase, and decreases when these pathways slow down. If the cell produces more ATP than it needs, the ATP inhibits the action of **phosphofructokinase**, slowing the rate of glycolysis.

The rates of glycolysis and the citric acid cycle are synchronised by the inhibition of phosphofructokinase by citrate. If citrate accumulates, glycolysis slows down. When citrate consumption increases, glycolysis increases the supply of acetyl groups to the citric acid cycle. This is shown in **Figure 1.44**.

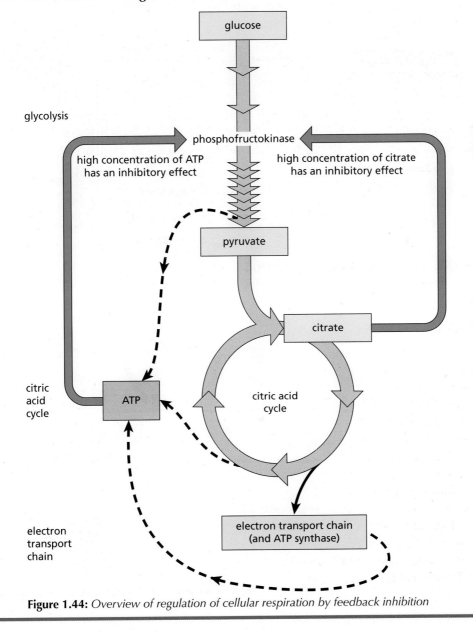

Figure 1.44: *Overview of regulation of cellular respiration by feedback inhibition*

Energy systems in muscle cells

Creatine phosphate

During strenuous muscle activity the cell rapidly breaks down its reserves of ATP to release energy. Muscle cells have an additional source of energy in **creatine phosphate** that can be used to replenish ATP supplies during rigorous bouts of exercise.

Creatine phosphate breaks down to release energy and phosphate that is used to convert ADP to ATP at a fast rate. This is shown in **Figure 1.45**. This system can only support strenuous muscle activity for around 10 seconds, when the creatine phosphate supply runs out. When muscle energy demand is low, ATP from cellular respiration is used to restore the levels of creatine phosphate.

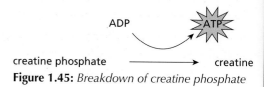

Figure 1.45: *Breakdown of creatine phosphate*

During vigorous exercise, the muscle cells do not get sufficient oxygen to support the electron transport chain. Under these conditions, pyruvate is converted to lactate. This converts hydrogen produced from the NADH during glycolysis to pyruvate to produce lactate. This regenerates the NAD needed to maintain ATP production through glycolysis. Lactate accumulates in muscle causing **fatigue**. This process is shown in **Figure 1.46**.

The **oxygen debt** is repaid when exercise is complete allowing respiration to provide the energy to convert lactate back to pyruvate and glucose in the liver.

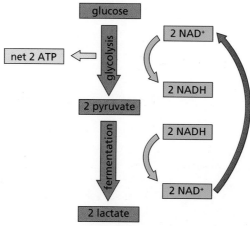

Figure 1.46: *Fermentation in animal cells*

Types of skeletal muscle fibres

Slow twitch (type 1) muscle fibres are good for endurance activities like long distance running. Slow twitch muscle fibres rely on aerobic respiration to generate ATP and have many mitochondria, a large blood supply and a high concentration of the oxygen-storing protein **myoglobin**. The major storage fuel of slow twitch muscle fibres is fats.

Fast twitch (type 2) muscle fibres are good for activities like sprinting. Fast twitch muscle fibres can only generate ATP through glycolysis. They have few mitochondria and a lower blood supply than slow twitch muscle fibres. The major storage fuels of fast twitch muscle fibres are glycogen and creatine phosphate.

Slow twitch muscle fibres contract more slowly, but can sustain contractions for longer, and are therefore better for endurance activities. Fast twitch muscle fibres contract more quickly, over short periods, and are therefore better for activities which require short bursts of activity.

Most human muscle tissue contains a mixture of both slow twitch and fast twitch muscle fibres. Athletes exhibit distinct patterns of muscle fibres which reflect their sporting activities.

Feature	Type of skeletal muscle fibre	
	Slow twitch (type 1)	Fast twitch (type 2)
activity most suitable for	endurance activities	sprinting/weightlifting
method of generating ATP	aerobic respiration	glycolysis only
mitochondria number	many	few
blood supply	large	lower
myoglobin present	yes	no
major storage fuels	fats	glycogen and creatine phosphate
contraction speed	slow	fast
contraction duration	long	short

GOT IT? ☐ ☐ ☐

End of Unit Assessment

Key area 1 – Division and differentiation in human cells

1. (a) Draw lines to match each of the following terms with its correct description. (3)

Term	Description
Stem cell	A mass of abnormal cells
Tumour	Gamete (such as sperm or ovum)
Germline cell	Unspecialised somatic cell that can divide to make copies of itself (self-renew) and/or differentiate into specialised cells

(b) State **one** current therapeutic use of stem cells. (1)

Key area 2 – Structure and replication of DNA

2. The following diagram shows two strands of DNA.

   (a) Name bond X. (1)

   (b) Name molecules Y and Z. (2)

   (c) Name the base which is complementary to cytosine. (1)

   (d) State the other **two** bases found in DNA. (2)

   (e) State the term used to describe the arrangement of the two DNA strands shown. (1)

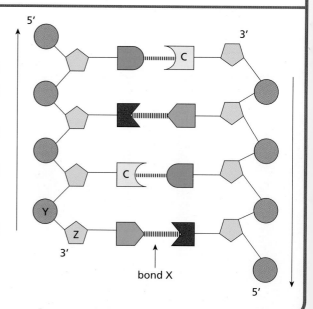

Key area 3 – Gene expression

3. Decide if each of the following statements about the structure of DNA and RNA is **True** or **False** and tick (✔) the correct box.

   If the answer is **False**, write the correct word(s) in the **Correction** box to replace the word <u>underlined</u> in the statement. (3)

Statement	True	False	Correction
RNA is a <u>single</u>-stranded molecule.			
DNA contains the base <u>uracil</u>.			
An RNA nucleotide contains a base, a phosphate and a <u>deoxyribose</u> sugar.			

4. The diagram below shows a strand of RNA during protein synthesis.

   (a) Name X1 and Y1. (2)

   (b) State the name of process Z. (1)

   (c) State the location of transcription within the cell. (1)

   (d) Give an example of post-translational modification. (1)

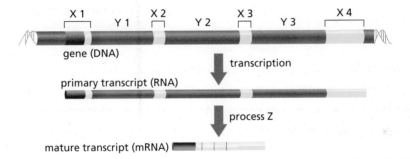

Key area 4 – Genes and proteins in health and disease

5. An original DNA base sequence is shown below.

    ATG CGT ACG

    The table below shows three mutations.

    Complete the table by inserting the names of the single gene mutations and if they cause a frameshift mutation by inserting yes or no.   (3)

Single gene mutation	DNA base sequence	Frameshift mutation (yes/no)
	ATG CGT CCG	
	ATC GCG TAC	
	ATG CTA CGC	

Key area 5 – Human genomics

6. The graph below shows the stages of PCR with time (minutes) vs. temperature (°C).

    (a) State the purpose of PCR.   (1)

    (b) Explain the purpose of heating in stage 1.   (1)

    (c) Describe the function of the primers used in stage 2.   (1)

    (d) Name the enzyme used in stage 3.   (1)

    (e) If one cycle takes 4.5 minutes, calculate the number of molecules of DNA that were produced after 45 minutes from one original DNA strand.   (1)

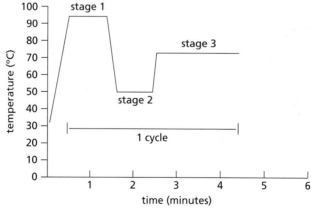

Key area 6 – Metabolic pathways

7. The diagram below shows a metabolic pathway.

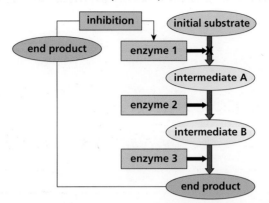

(a) This metabolic pathway requires energy. State the term used for this kind of pathway. (1)

(b) The end product inhibits enzyme 1 by attaching to its active site. State the term given to this type of inhibition. (1)

(c) Predict the effect of increasing the concentration of the end product on the concentration of intermediate B. (1)

(d) State the term given to this kind of inhibition. (1)

Key area 7 – Cellular respiration

8. The diagram below shows the three stages of cellular respiration.

   (a) Name stage X. (1)

   (b) Name molecule Z. (1)

   (c) Describe the effect of a high concentration of ATP or citrate being produced on cellular respiration. (1)

   (d) Name **one** other respiratory substrate which could be used instead of glucose. (1)

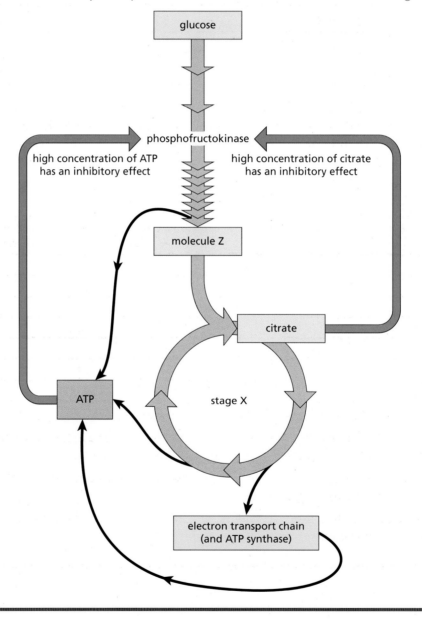

Key area 8 – Energy systems in muscle cells

9. The table below states some of the features of slow twitch and fast twitch skeletal muscle fibres. Complete the table by filling in the appropriate words in each empty box. (5)

Feature	Type of skeletal muscle fibre	
	Slow twitch (type 1)	Fast twitch (type 2)
activity most suitable for		
myoglobin present		
major storage fuels		
contraction speed		
contraction duration		

10. An experiment was carried out to investigate the effect of different glucose concentrations on the rate of respiration in yeast. Methylene blue will change from blue to colourless as the yeast respires. The time taken will depend upon the rate of respiration in the yeast.

    The results are shown below.

Glucose concentration (%)	Time taken for methylene blue to change from blue to colourless (seconds)
1	90
2	64
3	59
4	52
5	46
6	38
7	30

(a) State a conclusion that can be made from these results. (1)

(b) Calculate the percentage decrease for time taken for methylene blue to change to colourless between glucose concentrations of 1% and 7%. (1)

(c) Predict the time taken for methylene blue to change to colourless if the glucose concentration was increased to 8%. (1)

(d) Between which two glucose concentrations did the time taken for methylene blue to change to colourless decrease by the least? (1)

The structure and function of reproductive organs and gametes and their role in fertilisation

Gamete production and fertilisation

Male reproductive system

Gametes are produced in the testes (**Figure 2.1**) from **germline cells** by meiotic division, which reduces the diploid number to the haploid number of chromosomes.

Within the testes are the coiled **seminiferous tubules** where sperm production takes place (**Figure 2.2**). Between the seminiferous tubules are **interstitial cells** which produce the male hormone **testosterone**, which is transported in the bloodstream. In addition to stimulating sperm production,

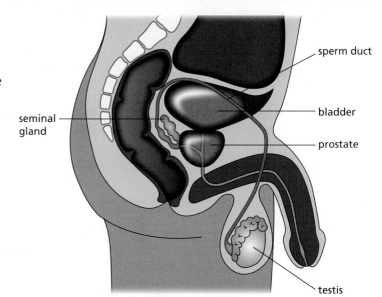

Figure 2.1: *Structure of male reproductive system*

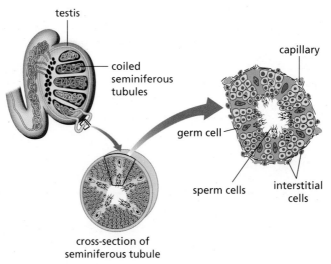

Figure 2.2: *Internal structure of testis*

testosterone also promotes the development of secondary sexual characteristics such as deepening voice and facial hair. Testosterone acts on two **accessory glands** called the **prostate gland** and the **seminal vesicle**. The action of these accessory organs produces fluids which, when added to the sperm, are collectively called **semen**. Secretions from the seminal vesicles are rich in sugars (especially fructose) which feed the sperm. The fluid also has clotting properties that make the semen sticky, ensuring that the semen clings inside the vagina long enough for the sperm to travel to the egg. **Prostaglandins** stimulate the uterus to contract. The prostate gland secretes enzymes which keep the semen at the correct fluidity.

Female reproductive system

In females, eggs develop by meiosis from germline cells in the ovaries, as shown in **Figure 2.3**.

Two important female hormones are produced in the ovaries, **oestrogen** and **progesterone**. The developing egg is surrounded by a cluster of cells known as a **follicle**, shown in **Figure 2.4**.

TOP TIP

Contractions of the female reproductive tract by the action of prostaglandins help move sperm towards the oviduct.

The follicle is a small cellular sac which secretes oestrogen. It eventually develops into a **corpus luteum**, which secretes progesterone.

If an egg is fertilised in the oviduct to produce a zygote, the zygote will then divide mitotically forming a **blastocyst**. It then moves down the oviduct aided by peristaltic waves and the action of the ciliated lining towards the uterus, where it may implant into the **endometrium**, eventually developing into an embryo.

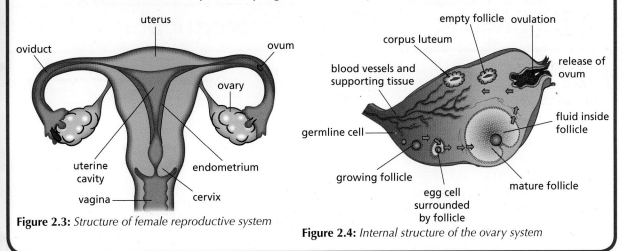

Figure 2.3: *Structure of female reproductive system*

Figure 2.4: *Internal structure of the ovary system*

Hormonal control of reproduction

Hormonal onset of puberty

Puberty results in several changes which increase the ability of an individual to reproduce. Some of these secondary sexual changes in males have been mentioned earlier. In females they involve the development of the reproductive organs and the start of the **menstrual cycle**. At this time, the **hypothalamus** in the brain, shown in **Figure 2.5**, secretes a hormone which triggers the **pituitary gland**. The pituitary gland then secretes **follicle-stimulating hormone (FSH)**, **luteinising hormone** and **interstitial cell-stimulating hormone (ICSH)**.

These hormones bring about the menstrual cycle in women and sperm production in men.

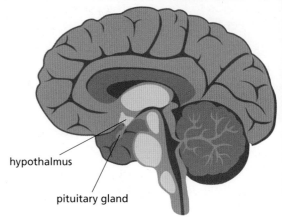

hypothalmus

pituitary gland

Figure 2.5: *Brain showing positions of hypothalamus and pituitary gland*

Hormonal control of sperm production

In males the hypothalamus secretes a releaser hormone which stimulates the pituitary gland to release both follicle-stimulating hormone and interstitial cell-stimulating hormone (**Figure 2.6**). These two hormones act on the testis by triggering the release of testosterone and the production of sperm cells. The secretion of the hormones is under **negative feedback control** where a high blood level of testosterone inhibits both follicle-stimulating hormone and interstitial cell-stimulating hormone production by the pituitary gland. This leads to a decrease in the blood level of testosterone which then stimulates the pituitary gland to start secreting more follicle-stimulating hormone and interstitial cell-stimulating hormone.

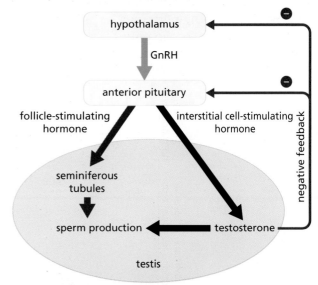

hypothalamus

GnRH

anterior pituitary

follicle-stimulating hormone

interstitial cell-stimulating hormone

negative feedback

seminiferous tubules

sperm production

testosterone

testis

Figure 2.6: *Negative feedback involved in the production of sperm*

TOP TIP

There are several bodily functions which are regulated by negative feedback, such as temperature control and blood sugar levels.

Hormonal control of the menstrual cycle

The menstrual cycle

In females the events surrounding ovulation and the changes in the endometrium are called the menstrual cycle. **Menstruation** takes place on the first day of the cycle. As shown in **Figure 2.7**, increasing levels of follicle-stimulating hormone secreted by the pituitary gland promotes the development of ovarian follicles and the secretion of oestrogen. Increasing levels of luteinising hormone, also secreted by the pituitary gland, causes ovulation and the development of the corpus luteum, which in turn secretes progesterone.

There are two phases of the menstrual cycle called the **follicular phase** and the **luteal phase**. These phases, shown in **Figure 2.8**, have profound effects on the ovaries.

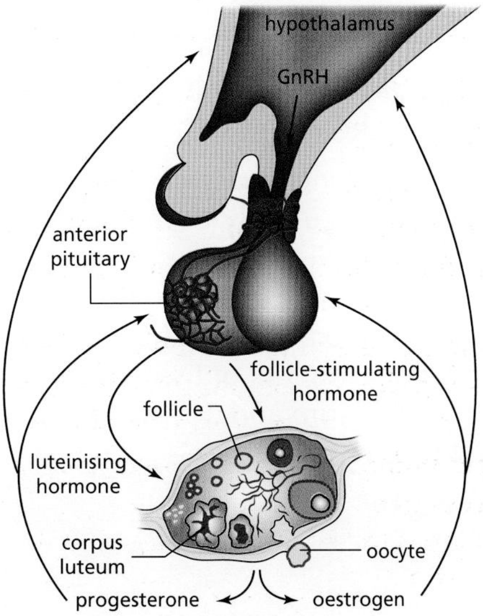

Figure 2.7: *Hormonal control of the menstrual cycle*

The follicular phase

In the follicular phase (**Figure 2.9**), follicle-stimulating hormone secreted by the pituitary gland causes the maturation of a follicle and the secretion of oestrogen from the ovaries. The increased level of oestrogen restores the wall of the endometrium after the bleeding associated with the last menstrual cycle. It also decreases the density of the mucus at the cervix, making it easier for sperm to swim through. As the oestrogen levels rise, the pituitary gland is stimulated to release luteinising hormone starting ovulation around the fourteenth day of the menstrual cycle.

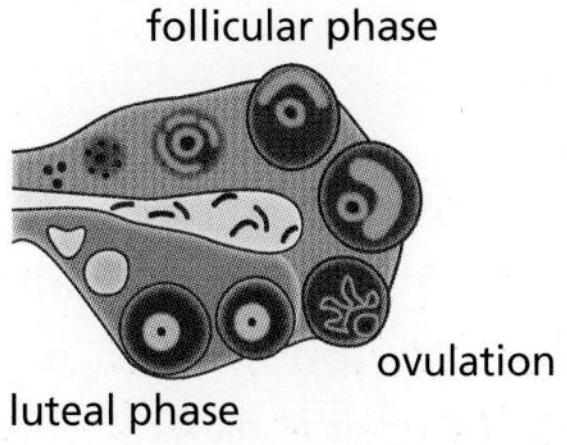

Figure 2.8: *Two different phases of the menstrual cycle*

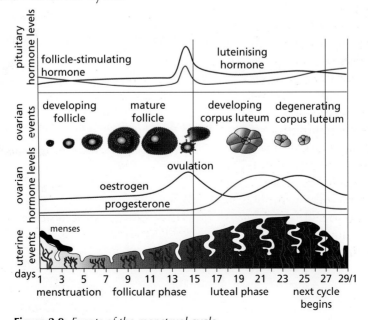

Figure 2.9: *Events of the menstrual cycle*

The luteal phase

In the luteal phase, luteinising hormone promotes the development of the corpus luteum. The corpus luteum secretes progesterone and oestrogen of increasing thickness into the wall of the endometrium, increasing the density of the mucus at the cervix. During this stage, the increased levels of progesterone and oestrogen have a negative feedback on the pituitary gland, which decreases the secretion of both luteinising hormone and follicle-stimulating hormone so that no new follicles are matured.

If the ovum is not fertilised, the corpus luteum usually degenerates so that the levels of progesterone and oestrogen fall. This in turn triggers the next menstrual cycle to start with the loss of tissue from the endometrium and 30–40 cm³ of blood (**Figure 2.10**).

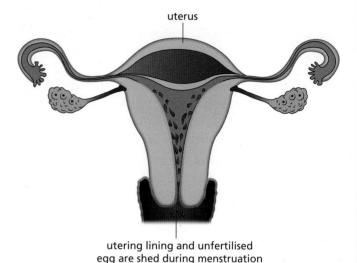

utering lining and unfertilised egg are shed during menstruation

Figure 2.10: *Menstrual flow of blood*

If fertilisation does take place, the onset of the next menstrual cycle is prevented by a hormone secreted by the zygote which mimics the effect of luteinising hormone. When this happens the corpus luteum is not able to degenerate but is maintained and continues to produce progesterone. The zygote develops into a blastocyst (**Figure 2.11**), which becomes implanted around seven days after fertilisation in the endometrium to develop into an embryo. The continued production of progesterone is taken over by the placenta.

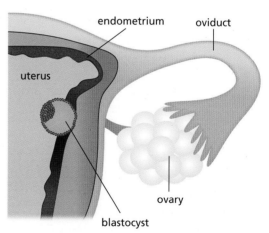

Figure 2.11: *Menstrual flow of blood*

Hormones associated with the menstrual cycle

Hormone	Where secreted	Effect of hormone
releaser hormone	hypothalamus	stimulates pituitary gland to secrete both follicle-stimulating hormone and luteinising hormone
follicle-stimulating hormone	pituitary gland	rising level of follicle-stimulating hormone stimulates maturation of follicle and production of oestrogen
luteinising hormone	pituitary gland	rising level of luteinising hormone stimulates mature follicle to rupture and release egg and form the corpus luteum, which secretes progesterone
oestrogen	ovary and follicle	repair and growth of endometrium negative effect on secretion of follicle-stimulating hormone and luteinising hormone
progesterone	ovary and corpus luteum	thickening of endometrium negative effect on pituitary gland activity causing less luteinising hormone to be secreted, which causes the corpus luteum to degenerate with less progesterone and oestrogen triggering the next menstrual flow

The biology of controlling fertility

Infertility treatments

Fertility may be affected by a number of factors, shown in **Figure 2.12**, acting singly or in combination, resulting in an inability to reproduce successfully.

Treatment of infertility is based on an understanding of the reproductive process.

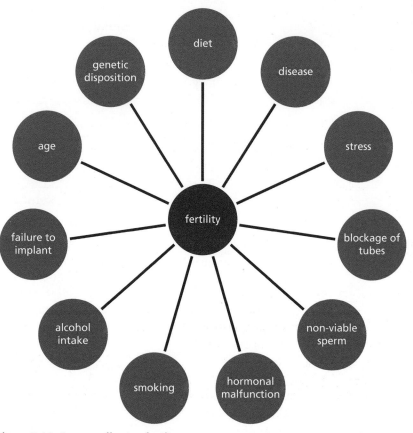

Figure 2.12: *Factors affecting fertility*

Fertile periods

In males, the blood levels of follicle-stimulating hormone and interstitial cell-stimulating hormone remain within narrow limits. Consequently, the concentration of testosterone does not change much and therefore sperm production remains consistent resulting in an ability to reproduce at any time. This is called **continuous fertility**.

In contrast, a female's reproductive potential is linked to a cycle of events meaning that she can only conceive within three to five days of ovulation, known as the **fertile period** (**Figure 2.13**). During ovulation the body temperature drops slightly then increases. Females have a fertility which is **cyclical**.

Sperm are able to survive for several days after intercourse, which means that they can potentially still fertilise an ovum if ovulation takes place while the sperm are still present and viable.

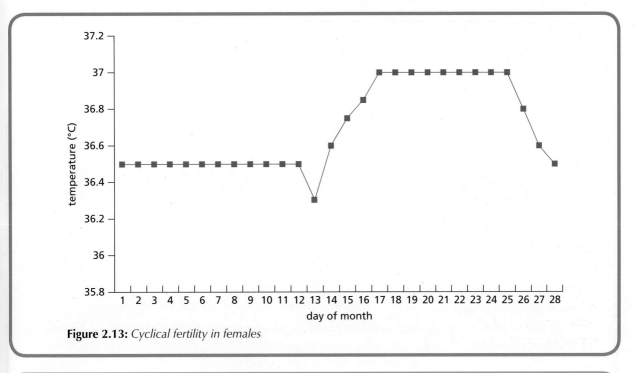

Figure 2.13: *Cyclical fertility in females*

Treatments for infertility

1. If infertility is due to a failure to ovulate, perhaps due to a lack of follicle-stimulating hormone or luteinising hormone, drugs which mimic the actions of these hormones can prevent the negative feedback effect of oestrogen on the pituitary gland's ability to secrete follicle-stimulating hormone or luteinising hormone. These ovulatory drugs can, however, provoke the release of more than one ovum, which can result in a multiple birth. This is called a **super ovulation**.

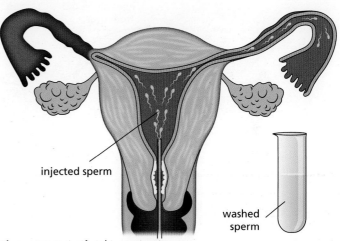

Figure 2.14: *Artificial insemination*

2. **Artificial insemination**, shown in **Figure 2.14**, introduces sperm into the female reproductive tract using an artificial means instead of sexual intercourse. If the male partner is **sterile**, the sperm can come from a donor.

3. A relatively new technique, shown in **Figure 2.15**, called **intracytoplasmic sperm injection (ICSI)** uses only one sperm to fertilise one ovum. It is used where there is an issue with either the number and/or viability of the sperm. A glass needle is used to inject the sperm head, containing the nucleus, directly into the ovum.

4. **In vitro fertilisation**, shown in **Figure 2.16**, allows the process of sperm and ova fusing to take place outside the female reproductive tract. It involves the removal of ova from the ovaries after hormone treatment then allowing them to mix with sperm in a culture dish. Any fertilised eggs can be incubated until they divide to reach a stage when they can be inserted into the uterus

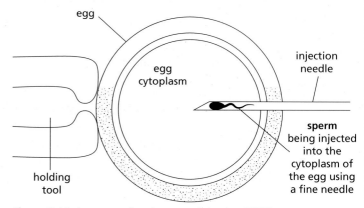

Figure 2.15: *Intracytoplasmic sperm injection [ICSI]*

with the aim that one or more will implant. A pre-implantation genetic diagnosis can be carried out to check for any single-gene disorders or chromosomal abnormalities. Unused embryos can be frozen and stored then used later.

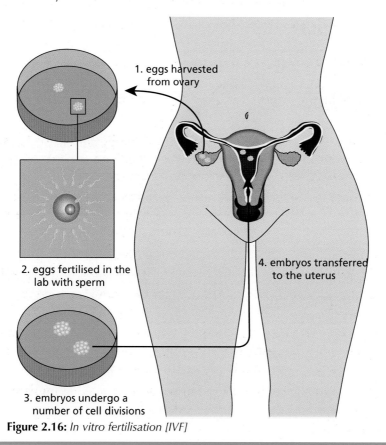

Figure 2.16: *In vitro fertilisation [IVF]*

Contraception

Contraception is the deliberate prevention of conception and can be either physical or chemical. Physical methods prevent sperm and egg meeting. Chemical methods use synthetic hormones which mimic the effects of those produced naturally.

Physical methods of contraception	
Method	*Description*
tubal ligation	surgical procedure, usually irreversible, in which the oviducts are cut and sealed so that ova cannot reach uterus
intrauterine device	small copper or plastic device inserted into the uterus to prevent implantation
cervical cap	device which fits tightly over the cervix preventing sperm reaching ova
diaphragm	soft rubber dome inserted into the vagina to prevent sperm reaching ova
vasectomy	surgical procedure, usually irreversible, in which the sperm ducts are cut and sealed preventing sperm from entering semen
condom	thin rubber cover which goes over erect penis preventing sperm from entering vagina
rhythm method	natural method which avoids intercourse during fertile period

Chemical methods of contraception	
Method	*Description*
oral contraceptive pill	synthetic versions of the hormones progesterone and oestrogen which have the same negative feedback properties on the secretions of the pituitary gland
morning after pill	used in circumstances when no other method of contraception was available at the time of sexual intercourse or if the original method of contraception failed
	contains very high levels of the synthetic forms of progesterone and oestrogen delaying ovulation and inhibiting implantation
	also causes thickening of the mucus around the cervix making it difficult for sperm to penetrate
mini pill	contains only the synthetic version of progesterone causing negative feedback on the pituitary gland as well as an increased thickening of the cervical mucus
	also causes the endometrium to thin making implantation difficult

Antenatal and postnatal screening

Antenatal screening

Antenatal (prenatal) screening is a method of detecting potential issues with an embryo or fetus before birth. For example, where there is a family history of a genetic condition. The number of conditions which can be detected before birth is increasing all the time. The majority of the techniques used are non-invasive and are used during the first six months of pregnancy. Antenatal testing can reveal the sex of the developing embryo as well as its blood group. The screening will also indicate the delivery date.

Ultrasound imaging

Ultrasound imaging, shown in **Figure 2.17**, makes use of high-frequency sound waves passed through the abdominal wall to create an image of the fetus in the uterus. This reveals the size, age and position of the fetus, and helps indicate if there are any abnormalities in the skeleton and organs.

Not all potential birth defects can be detected by ultrasound imaging.

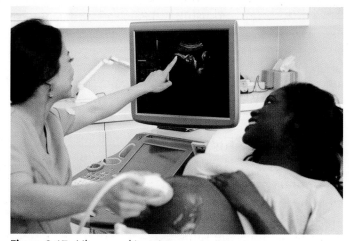

Figure 2.17: *Ultrasound imaging*

Biochemical testing

As pregnancy proceeds, the levels of proteins produced by the placenta can be tested by taking a blood sample, as shown in **Figure 2.18**.

For example, unusually low levels of the protein **alpha-fetoprotein** can help identify fetuses with Down's syndrome.

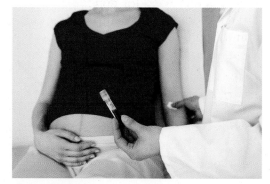

Figure 2.18: *Blood sample to be used for biochemical testing*

Diagnostic testing

Diagnostic tests involve taking a sample of either the placenta, the amniotic fluid or fetal blood. The samples are then sent away and examined in a laboratory for chromosomal or genetic abnormalities. The two main diagnostic tests are **amniocentesis** and **chorionic villus** sampling.

Amniocentesis

Amniocentesis, shown in **Figure 2.19,** is used to diagnose potential congenital abnormalities by examining cells found in the amniotic fluid. This takes place between the fifteenth and twentieth weeks of pregnancy and is offered to women over the age of 35 or who have already had a blood test indicating potential abnormalities. A small sample of the **amniotic fluid** which surrounds the fetus is removed using a long thin needle inserted through the abdominal wall. The amniotic fluid contains cells shed by the fetus which are used for genetic analysis. This technique can help detect possible defects in the development of the brain or spinal cord.

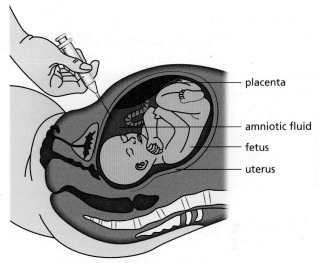

Figure 2.19: *Amniocentesis*

Chorionic villus sampling

Chorionic villus sampling, **Figure 2.20**, is used to diagnose potential congenital abnormalities by examining cells from the placenta. This takes place between the tenth and thirteenth weeks of pregnancy and is offered to women who have a family history of a genetic condition or have already had a blood test indicating potential abnormalities. Cells containing the same genetic material as the developing fetus are removed from the placenta. A long flexible tube is inserted through the vagina into the cervix. It is then guided towards the placenta and the chorionic villi, shown in **Figure 2.21**.

A small sample of tissue is taken from the placenta and used for genetic analysis. Unlike amniocentesis, this technique cannot help detect possible defects in the development of the brain or spinal cord.

Both types of diagnostic testing carry a risk of inducing a miscarriage. The risk in amniocentesis is approximately 1% after the fifteenth week of pregnancy. The risk of miscarriage in chorionic villus sampling is estimated to be 1–2%.

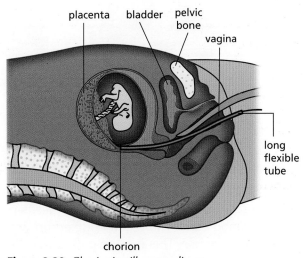

Figure 2.20: *Chorionic villus sampling*

Cells taken by amniocentesis and/or chorionic villus sampling can be used to produce a representation of the chromosomes present in the cells of a baby, known as a **karyotype** (**Figure 2.22**).

Any abnormalities in terms of the numbers and/or shapes of the chromosomes can help diagnose genetic conditions like Down's syndrome.

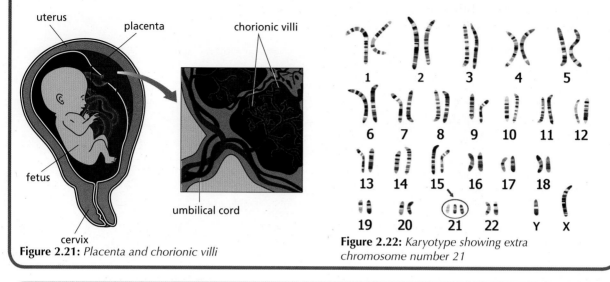

Figure 2.21: *Placenta and chorionic villi*

Figure 2.22: *Karyotype showing extra chromosome number 21*

Rhesus antibody testing

In a normal pregnancy, the blood of the mother and fetus are kept apart by the barrier of the placenta. The immune system of the mother will not detect the presence of a foreign agent in that half of the genetic material of the fetus belonging to the father, and so the fetus will have protein markers which are termed **antigenic**. One marker is called the **rhesus factor**. People who have this marker are termed rhesus-positive and those who don't are rhesus-negative (**Figure 2.23**).

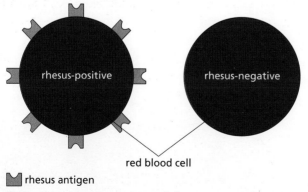

red blood cell

▉ rhesus antigen

Figure 2.23: *Rhesus-positive and rhesus-negative blood*

TOP TIP

Approximately 85% of the population are rhesus-positive.

Sensitisation

If a rhesus-negative mother carries a rhesus-positive baby then during birth some of the baby's blood cells will become mixed up with the mother's blood cells and set up an immune response. This is known as a **sensitisation** event. This becomes serious if the mother goes on to have a second baby which is rhesus-positive. Antibodies from the mother can pass across the placenta into the newborn baby and destroy its red blood cells causing anaemia. This is shown in **Figure 2.24**.

It is possible to treat this situation by giving the mother a massive dose of anti-rhesus antibodies after birth. The mother's immune system is prevented from encountering the rhesus antigen. In addition the baby can be given a blood transfusion while it is still in the uterus via a vein in the umbilical cord, as shown in **Figure 2.25**.

| rhesus-negative woman and rhesus-positive man conceive a child | rhesus-negative woman with rhesus-positive fetus | cells from rhesus-positive fetus enter woman's bloodstream | woman becomes sensitised-antibodies (+) form to fight rhesus-positive blood cells | in the next rhesus-positive pregnancy, maternal antibodies attack fetal red blood cells |

Figure 2.24: *Sensitisation of rhesus-negative mother by rhesus-positive fetus*

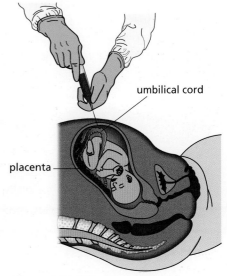

Figure 2.25: *Blood transfusion of unborn baby*

Postnatal screening

Postnatal screening is the use of diagnostic testing to check for any abnormalities in a baby after it is born.

One important use of screening is to check for an error in metabolism called **phenylketonuria**, which is caused by an **autosomal** recessive allele. Babies born in the UK are tested for this condition by taking a blood sample from the heel as shown in **Figure 2.26**.

If a baby is diagnosed with phenylketonuria then a low-protein diet avoiding foods such as potatoes and cereals is prescribed. Providing the diet is followed then the brain function of the baby will develop normally. The low-protein diet is usually continued into adulthood.

Patterns of inherited conditions can be shown by collecting data over several generations of a family to produce pedigree charts which reveal both the phenotypes and genotypes of family members. This information is useful if a family is known to be at high risk of a genetic condition such as albinism, Huntington's disease or haemophilia.

Figure 2.26: *Postnatal screening for phenylketonuria*

A pedigree chart, as shown in **Figure 2.27**, shows how a genetic trait is passed through several generations of a family. This is useful as a predictor of how likely an individual is to have or to develop such a genetic trait. It can be used to track how a genetic condition (particularly if it is an unusual one) is expressed over several generations, and provide increased knowledge on which to base decisions about having children.

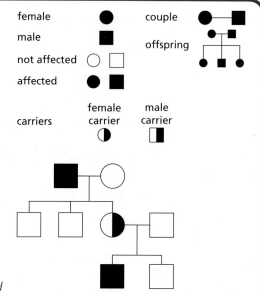

Figure 2.27: *Typical pedigree showing how a trait is inherited*

Inheritance patterns

Four important inheritance patterns can be shown using pedigree charts.

Defective recessive autosomal inheritance

A disorder such as albinism (**Figure 2.28**) which is caused by a defective recessive autosomal allele:

- is expressed relatively rarely
- usually skips generations
- affects both males and females in equal numbers
- requires the affected individual to be homozygous recessive
- can be carried by a heterozygous individual
- can result from two unaffected parents who are heterozygous.

Figure 2.28: *Pedigree of defective recessive autosomal inheritance*

Defective autosomal dominant allele

A disorder such as Huntington's disease (**Figure 2.29**) which is caused by a defective autosomal dominant allele:

- affects both males and females in equal numbers
- means anybody affected will have an affected parent
- no longer appears in future generations if a branch of the pedigree does show the disorder
- results in all non-affected individuals being homozygous recessive
- means anybody affected is either double dominant or heterozygous.

Figure 2.29: *Pedigree of defective dominant autosomal inheritance*

Autosomal defective allele

A disorder such as sickle-cell anaemia (**Figure 2.30**) which is caused by an autosomal defective allele:

- affects both males and females in equal numbers

- in the homozygous state produces the maximum expression of the phenotype

- is rarely expressed maximally

- in the heterozygous state produces a reduced expression of the phenotype.

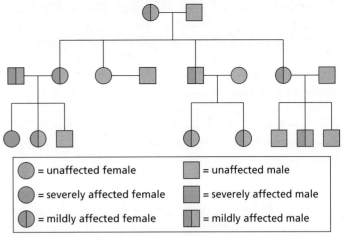

= unaffected female   = unaffected male

= severely affected female   = severely affected male

= mildly affected female   = mildly affected male

Figure 2.30: *Pedigree showing inheritance of sickle-cell anaemia*

Defective sex-linked recessive allele

A disorder such as haemophilia (**Figure 2.31**) which is caused by a defective sex-linked recessive allele:

- affects many more males than females

- is not transmitted to a male from his affected father

- needs an individual to be homozygous if they are female

- will be expressed in a male who has one copy of the defective allele

- will not be expressed in a homozygous or heterozygous female or a male who has the normal allele

- means usually the mother of an affected male is, herself, unaffected

- means all daughters of affected fathers will either be carriers or be affected themselves.

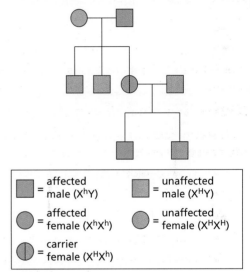

= affected male (X^hY)   = unaffected male (X^HY)

= affected female (X^hX^h)   = unaffected female (X^HX^H)

= carrier female (X^HX^h)

Figure 2.31: *Pedigree of defective sex-linked inheritance*

The structure and function of arteries, capillaries and veins

Circulatory system

Transport of important materials around the body depends on the action of the circulatory system, which consists of the heart and blood vessels, arteries, capillaries and veins, as shown in **Figure 2.32**. The heart pumps the blood through arteries, capillaries then veins before returning it back to the heart.

Within the blood vessels is a space called the central lumen through which blood travels. The **central lumen** is lined with special cells which form a smooth layer called the **endothelium**. Each of the three main types of blood vessels has a different coat on the outside of the endothelium related to its function.

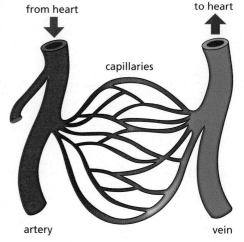

Figure 2.32: *Artery and vein connected by capillaries*

Arteries

Arteries are vessels which carry blood away from the heart. Their walls, **Figure 2.33**, are adapted to withstand the very high pressure of blood which is a result of the muscular contractions of the heart.

These walls consist of three layers: the inner endothelium, a middle layer which consists of smooth muscle and elastic fibres, and a strong outer layer which consists of connective tissue, collagen and elastic tissue. The muscular wall of an artery can recoil as a wave of pressure passes through.

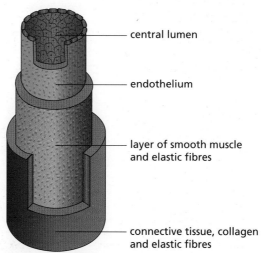

Figure 2.33: *Walls of an artery*

The smooth muscle in the arterial wall is capable of relaxing (**vasodilation**) or contracting (**vasoconstriction**) in response to different demands, as shown in **Figure 2.34**. For example, in cold weather, the blood vessels near the skin can vasoconstrict causing less radiative heat loss, while strenuous exercise can cause these blood vessels to vasodilate to allow more radiative heat loss.

TOP TIP

Radiative heat loss is linked to the autonomic nervous system studied later in this unit.

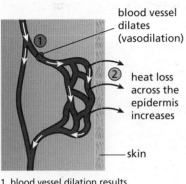 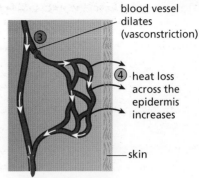

1. blood vessel dilation results in increased blood flow toward the surface of the skin
2. increased blood flow beneath the epidermis results in increased heat loss (blue arrows)

3. blood vessel constriction results in decreased blood flow toward the surface of the skin
4. decreased blood flow beneath the epidermis results in decreased heat loss

Figure 2.34: *Vasodilation and vasoconstriction in the skin*

Veins

Veins are blood vessels which return blood to the heart. The layer of muscle in the wall of a vein is much thinner than that of an artery since the blood flow is under much less pressure. The central lumen of a vein is usually much larger than that of an artery to allow blood to flow more easily back to the heart. To help the one-way flow of blood back to the heart, veins also have valves, as shown in **Figure 2.35**.

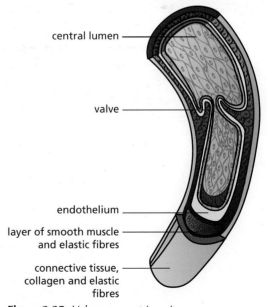

Figure 2.35: *Valves present in veins*

Capillaries

Blood travels through arteries towards veins via a dense network of tiny capillaries as shown in **Figure 2.36**.

The tiny arteries and veins are called arterioles and venules, respectively.

Exchange of materials such as nutrients, gases, fluids and wastes takes place across the one-cell thick walls of the capillaries.

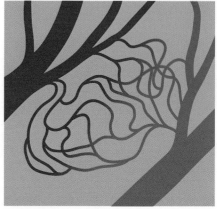

Figure 2.36: *Capillaries connect arterioles to venules*

Tissue fluid

When blood arrives at a capillary bed, the pressure forces some of the **plasma** (**Figure 2.37**) out through the thin walls into the space outside.

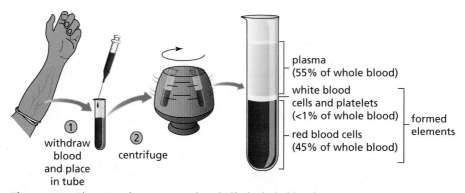

Figure 2.37: *Plasma makes up more than half of whole blood*

> **TOP TIP**
>
> Plasma contains many dissolved substances such as glucose, amino acids, carbon dioxide, oxygen, urea, vitamins, minerals, hormones and antibodies.

This is called **tissue fluid** and is similar to plasma but contains no protein molecules (**Figure 2.38**). Tissue fluid allows exchange of materials between capillaries and tissue cells.

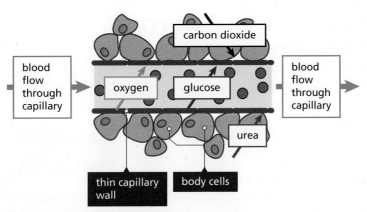

Figure 2.38: *Tissue fluid formation*

Not all the tissue fluid returns back to the capillary. Instead it enters the lymphatic system (**Figure 2.39**) via lymphatic vessels. These are unusual in that they are closed at one end. Lymph collected from all the lymphatic vessels eventually re-enters blood circulation.

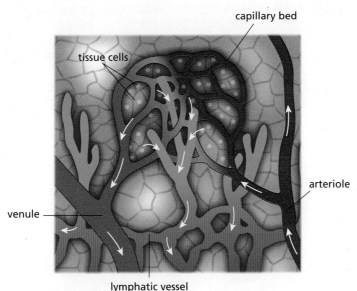

Figure 2.39: *The lymphatic system*

The structure and function of the heart

Cardiac function and output

Blood is pumped through the circulatory system by the heart, entering by the two atria and leaving from the two ventricles, as shown in **Figure 2.40**. The right side deals with deoxygenated blood while the left side deals with oxygenated blood. Valves prevent backflow so that the blood travels in one direction.

> **TOP TIP**
>
> The average body contains about five litres of blood, which means that all of our blood is pumped through our hearts about once every minute.

One measurement associated with heart function is the **cardiac output**, the volume of blood pumped by either the left or right ventricle per minute. Both left and right ventricles pump the same volume of blood through the aorta and pulmonary arteries. The cardiac output is calculated from the heart rate and **stroke volume**:

cardiac output = heart rate x stroke volume

The cardiac output of an untrained adult with a resting heart rate of 72 beats per minute and a stroke volume of 70 cm³/minute will be 5040 cm³/minute. A highly trained athlete's cardiac output can be eight times this figure, due to the efficiency of their heart function.

> **TOP TIP**
>
> When you exercise, cardiac output increases to meet the increasing demand for oxygen, glucose and the removal of carbon dioxide.

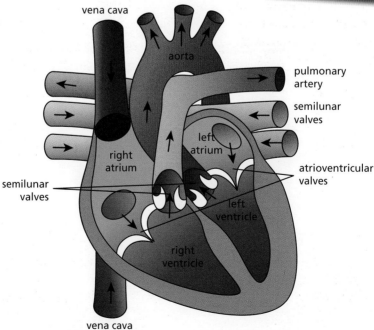

Figure 2.40: *Structure of heart and associated blood vessels*

Cardiac cycle

Each single beat of the heart, lasting on average about 0.8 seconds, is made up of a sequence of highly co-ordinated events known as the **cardiac cycle**, consisting of two phases (**Figure 2.41**):

1. Relaxation phase known as **diastole** when the heart muscle is relaxed and the heart fills up with blood.

2. Contraction phase known as **systole** when the heart muscle is contracted and blood is forced from the atria into the ventricles and from the ventricles out of the heart.

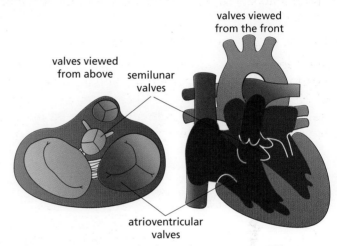

Figure 2.41: *Two phases of the cardiac cycle*

Linked to these two different phases is the action of the valves in the heart. The **atrioventricular valves** are found between the two atria and the two ventricles. The **semilunar valves** are located at the exit of the ventricles (**Figure 2.42**).

As shown in **Figure 2.43**, when atrial systole starts, the blood remaining in the atria is pumped into the two ventricles through the now open atrioventricular valves. When the ventricles go into systole almost immediately after atrial systole, they are closed and the semilunar valves are forced open to allow blood to travel out into the aorta and pulmonary artery. The entire sequence of events which make up the cardiac cycle, as shown in **Figure 2.44**, takes place in less than one second.

valves viewed from above

valves viewed from the front

semilunar valves

atrioventricular valves

Figure 2.42: *Location of valves in heart*

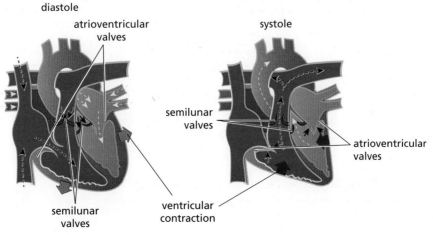

diastole

atrioventricular valves

systole

semilunar valves

atrioventricular valves

semilunar valves

ventricular contraction

Figure 2.43: *Diastole and systole*

This consists of contraction and relaxation of the heart muscle, systole and diastole, and the smooth operation of the valves to ensure the one-way flow of blood in and out of the heart.

As the valves open and close in pairs they make a characteristic sound known as 'lubb' and 'dup' (**Figure 2.45**).

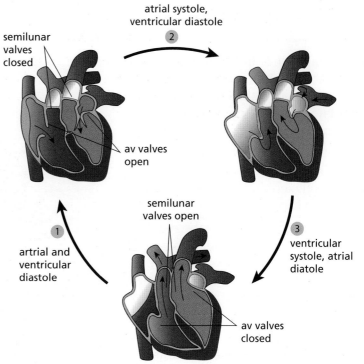

Figure 2.44: *Cardiac cycle*

TOP TIP

These two sounds are what are picked up by a stethoscope against the chest wall.

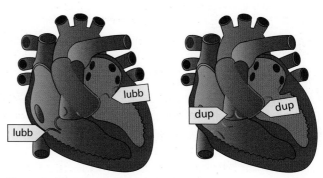

Figure 2.45: *Sounds of the heart in action*

Cardiac-conducting system

The heart muscle is unusual in that it can contract without an external nervous supply. This ability of heart muscle cells to generate their own stimulation ensures the whole heart contracts in a rhythmic and highly co-ordinated way using its own conducting system, as shown in **Figure 2.46**.

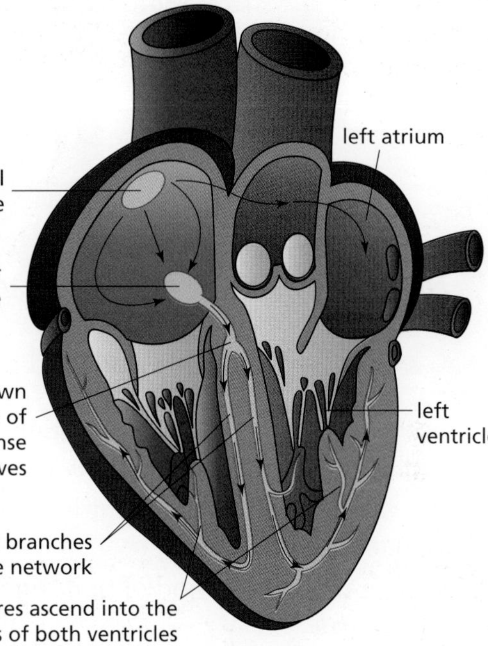

TOP TIP

Although the heart can set its own pace, the actual rate of heartbeat is highly variable and external nerve impulses can speed up or slow down this rate according to demands.

Figure 2.46: *Cardiac-conducting system of heart*

The beat is started in a **node** of nerve tissue called the pacemaker or **sinoatrial node** located at the top of the right atrium, which sets the rate of heartbeat. Electrical impulses from the sinoatrial node travel across the walls of the two atria causing them to contract almost simultaneously (atrial systole). These impulses are picked up by the **atrioventricular node** located near the lower centre of both atria. The atrioventricular node passes the incoming electrical impulses from the sinoatrial node down the middle of the heart and out to the ventricles causing them to contract simultaneously a fraction of a second after the atria (ventricular systole). This slight delay gives the atria time to contract and force their contents into the ventricles just before these start to contract.

The arrangement of the nerves from the atrioventricular node causes the ventricles to contract from the base upwards, squeezing out the blood into the aorta or pulmonary artery.

Electrocardiograms

The changes in the electrical activity of the heart as it functions can be recorded on a trace called an **electrocardiogram** (ECG), as shown in **Figure 2.47**.

A normal ECG consists of three connected waves identified by the letters P, QRS and T.

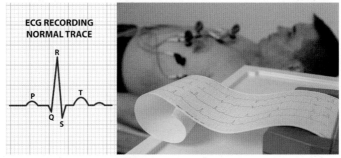

Figure 2.47: *Electrical activity of heart generating an electrocardiogram*

These waves are shown in **Figure 2.48** and described here:

- P wave – right and left atria are stimulated to contract. The P wave lasts less than 0.12 seconds
- QRS wave – right and left ventricles are stimulated to contract. The QRS wave lasts less than 0.10 seconds
- T wave – recovery period of both right and left ventricles. The T wave lasts about 0.25 seconds.

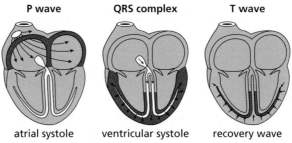

Figure 2.48: *P, QRS and T waves*

Change to this normal trace can indicate that the heart's function is not normal, as shown in **Figure 2.49**.

ventricles contracting more rapidly than normal

fast heartbeat

atria more rapidly than normal

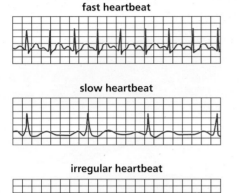

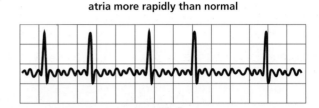

slow heartbeat

irregular heartbeat

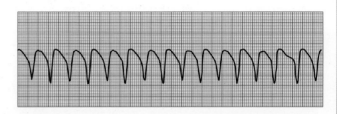

Figure 2.49: *Electrocardiagrams can reveal abnormal heart function*

The medulla in the brain has a number of functions, one of which is to regulate the activity of the sinoatrial node (**Figure 2.50**).

It does this through the action of the autonomic nervous system. Sympathetic nerve action increases the activity of the sinoatrial node causing the heart to beat faster and increase the cardiac output. Sympathetic nerve fibres are over almost all of the heart muscle. Parasympathetic activity has the opposite effect, slowing down the heartbeat and decreasing the cardiac output. These actions are **antagonistic** to each other and are mediated by two different neurotransmitters as shown in the table below.

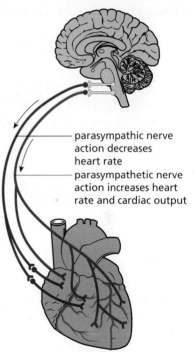

parasympathic nerve action decreases heart rate

parasympathetic nerve action increases heart rate and cardiac output

Figure 2.50: *Autonomic control of heartbeat*

Division of autonomic nervous system	Neurotransmitter secreted	Effect
parasympathetic	acetylcholine	heart, pulse rate and cardiac output decrease
sympathetic	nor-adrenaline (nor-epinephrine)	heart, pulse rate and cardiac output increase

Blood pressure changes

With each contraction of the left and right ventricles blood is forced into the arterial system under pressure (**Figure 2.51**).

Each contraction and relaxation gives rise to systolic and diastolic blood pressures, respectively. The maximum systolic pressure occurs when the ventricles exert maximum force on the blood, which falls to its minimum when the ventricles relax.

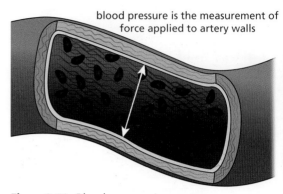

blood pressure is the measurement of force applied to artery walls

Figure 2.51: *Blood pressure in an artery*

Blood pressure is measured using a device called a **sphygmomanometer** (**Figure 2.52**).

This has an inflatable cuff which can temporarily stop the flow of blood back to the heart allowing measurement of the systolic pressure, typically around 120 mm Hg. The cuff is then deflated gradually restoring the blood flow allowing measurement of the diastolic pressure, typically around 70 mm Hg. It also provides the pulse rate in beats per minute.

Figure 2.52: *A sphygmomanometer measures blood pressure*

High blood pressure, **hypertension**, can be one of a number of risk factors in causing heart disease and strokes (**Figure 2.53**).

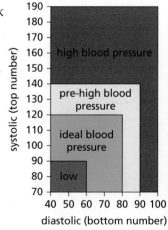

Figure 2.53: *Variations in blood pressure*

Lifestyle changes and the use of medication can help reduce high blood pressure to an ideal blood pressure for an individual.

The various changes which occur in the heart can be summarised in a chart showing pressure, volume, electrical activity and sound (**Figure 2.54**).

This is useful in detecting any abnormalities in muscle and valve functions.

TOP TIP

Make sure you understand all the traces featured in this graph and ask your teacher to explain anything you still aren't clear about.

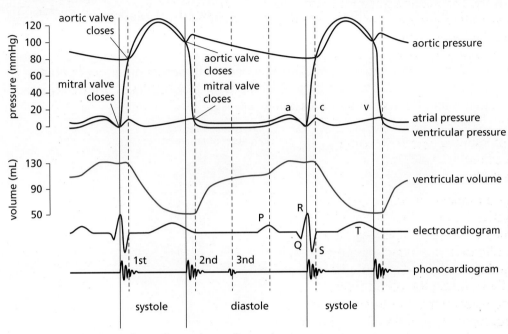

Figure 2.54: *Changes in heart during the cardiac cycle*

Pathology of cardiovascular disease (CVD)

Atherosclerosis

TOP TIP

The word atheroma comes from the Greek meaning porridge.

Depending on a number of factors such as age, lifestyle, diet, smoking and genetics, arteries can become clogged up with fatty substances which form an **atheroma**, as shown in **Figure 2.55**.

As the fatty deposits of atheroma build up, the central lumen of an artery becomes progressively narrower. This makes it more difficult for blood to pass through, increasing blood pressure and the risk of cardiovascular disease.

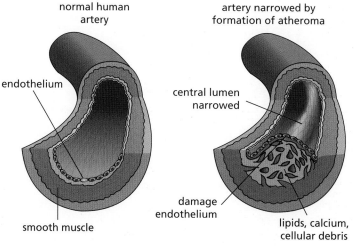

normal human artery

artery narrowed by formation of atheroma

endothelium

central lumen narrowed

damage endothelium

smooth muscle

lipids, calcium, cellular debris

Figure 2.55: *Formation of atheroma in an artery*

Thrombosis

As an atheroma builds up it becomes a site for the formation of a blood clot called a **thrombus**. Blood clotting is the process which prevents bleeding when a blood vessel is damaged. A series of reactions occurs to stop bleeding by forming a clot to act as a plug. The process starts with **prothrombin**, an inactive enzyme, being converted into its active form, **thrombin**. Thrombin converts **fibrinogen** into **fibrin** forming meshwork which traps blood platelets and blood cells creating a clot (**Figure 2.56**).

There is a risk the blood clot will be dislodged and become mobile, forming an **embolus** which can potentially block blood flowing to the heart resulting in a **myocardial infarction**.

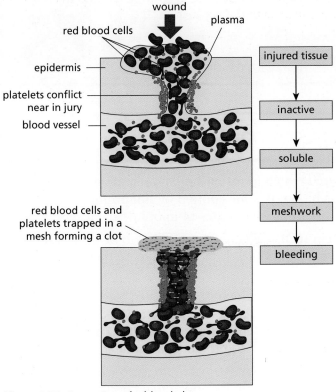

Figure 2.56: *Formation of a blood clot*

Causes of peripheral vascular disorders

Peripheral vascular disease occurs when the damage caused by narrowing of arteries takes place distant from the heart. One of the most common forms of peripheral vascular disease is **deep vein thrombosis**, when a blood clot forms in a deep vein, usually in a leg. Sometimes, part of the clot becomes detached to form an embolus resulting in a **pulmonary embolism**, as shown in **Figure 2.57**.

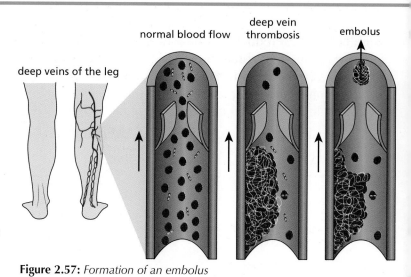

Figure 2.57: *Formation of an embolus*

Control of cholesterol levels

Cholesterol is an insoluble lipid which forms part of an animal cell membrane. Because cholesterol is insoluble in the blood, it is transported by **lipoproteins**, which are soluble in the blood and act as carriers. There are two types of lipoprotein carriers:

1. **Low-density lipoprotein (LDL)**, which is considered to be bad because it promotes the formation of atheroma. High levels of LDL increase the risk of cardiovascular disease.

2. **High-density lipoprotein (HDL)**, which is considered to be good because it helps remove LDL from the arteries by acting as a scavenger molecule, carrying the LDL back to the liver to be broken down and excreted. Up to one third of cholesterol is carried by HDL, which is believed to protect against heart attack and stroke.

LDL transports cholesterol to cells which have special receptors on their surface. The number of LDL receptors is directly affected by how much cholesterol is in each cell. As the level of cholesterol increases, the number of receptors falls. This reduction in LDL receptors means the LDL is forced to carry the excess cholesterol elsewhere, increasing the risk of atheroma forming in the endothelium of arteries. High levels of HDLs, in relation to LDLs, help to prevent this happening by mopping up the excess cholesterol and transporting it to the liver for eventual elimination.

Unusually high levels of cholesterol in the blood is called **hypercholesterolaemia** which can lead to an increased risk of developing cardiovascular disease and stroke, as shown in **Figure 2.58**. There is, in some people, a genetic link to this condition called **familial hypercholesterolaemia (FH)**. This is caused by an autosomal dominant defective allele which codes for a reduction in the number of LDL receptors or the synthesis of defective LDL receptors. A combination of a good lifestyle and possibly drugs called **statins** can reduce the level of blood cholesterol to a normal safe level.

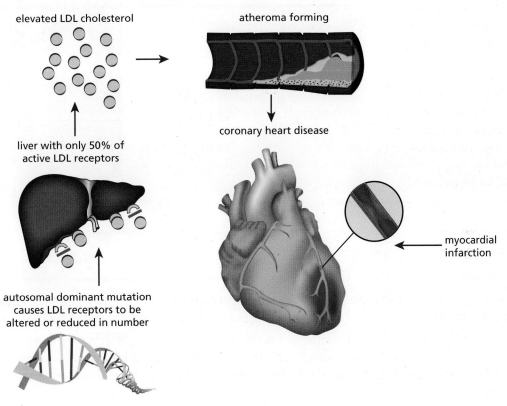

Figure 2.58: *High levels of cholesterol can lead to cardiovascular disease*

TOP TIP

There are several ways to reduce the level of LDLs and increase the level of HDLs. These include eating less animal fat and eating more fats found in fish, nuts, plant spreads and oils, eating more fruit, wholegrain food, beans and other legumes, taking regular exercise and giving up smoking.

Blood glucose levels and obesity

Blood glucose levels

High levels of blood glucose are now known to provoke atherosclerosis by damaging the endothelial lining of blood vessels and causing fatty streak formations. Elevated glucose levels cause phenotypic changes in the working of the endothelial cells, which absorb more glucose than normal so that the layer becomes thickened and sticky, leading to the formation of atheroma. Typically these high levels of blood glucose are linked to patients with diabetes.

The regulation of blood sugar levels is very carefully controlled within narrow limits using negative feedback (**Figure 2.59**).

Homeostasis

This maintains the concentration of glucose in the blood at the optimum and a steady state environment for cells to work properly. Such a mechanism

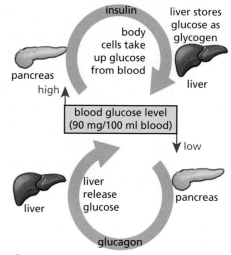

Figure 2.59: *Negative feedback control of blood glucose*

helps maintain **homeostasis** and any departure from the **set point** could well result in serious health issues. A rise above the set point is detected by cells in the pancreas which can secrete two different hormones to regulate the change. If the blood sugar goes above the set point, the pancreas secretes insulin which promotes the conversion of glucose to glycogen in the liver. If the blood sugar goes below the set point, glucagon is secreted which converts glycogen to glucose.

In a suddenly stressful situation, glucose is required very quickly to power the fight or flight response (**Figure 2.60**).

Figure 2.60: *Fight or flight reaction*

Adrenal glands

Situated above the kidneys, **adrenal glands** secrete adrenaline into the bloodstream, which supercharges the conversion of glycogen to glucose.

TOP TIP

Other examples of homeostasis include control of temperature, blood pH and breathing rates.

Individuals who suffer from diabetes are unable to regulate their blood glucose levels due to insufficient insulin being produced by the pancreas. There are two forms of diabetes:

1. Type 1 diabetes (previously known as juvenile diabetes) usually develops in young people, although it can develop in adults. The pancreas does not make enough insulin and daily injections of insulin are required, along with adopting a healthy lifestyle.

2. Type 2 diabetes (previously known as adult-onset diabetes) can affect people of any age, but usually emerges in middle-aged and elderly individuals. It is closely linked to obesity and has a strong genetic component. The pancreas continues to make insulin, but insulin receptors on the cells in the liver have become desensitised and less in number, and therefore don't readily convert glucose to glycogen. Treatment involves medication along with adopting a healthy lifestyle, including taking regular exercise.

Obesity

TOP TIP

Approximately one in four adults in the UK are obese.

Obesity in adults and children is of concern because it is linked to high blood pressure, type 2 diabetes, some forms of cancer and cardiovascular disease (**Figure 2.61**).

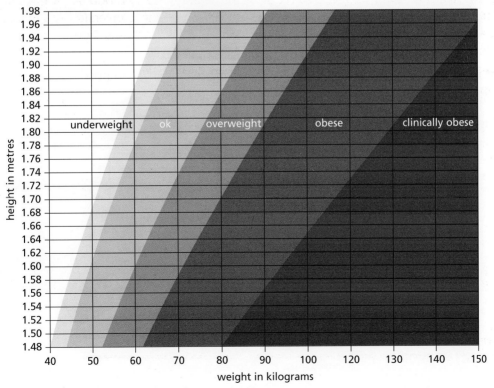

Figure 2.61: *Weight categories in relation to height measurements*

BMI

One of several ways of classifying obesity is the **body mass index (BMI)**, which is calculated:

$$\text{body weight (kg)} / [\text{height (m)}]^2$$

For adults a BMI score of 18.5–24.9 indicates a healthy weight. A BMI score of 25–29.9 indicates an individual is overweight. A BMI score of 30 or higher is classified as obese.

Another way of measuring obesity is by measuring the waist circumference (**Figure 2.62**). In men, a waist size of 94 cm or higher indicates an increased risk of obesity-related health issues. For women the equivalent waist size is 80 cm or higher.

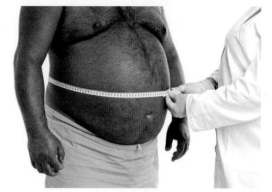

Figure 2.62: *Measurement of waist circumference*

Certain devices can measure the skinfold thickness in places such as the trunk, under the shoulder blade, and the front and back of arms and thighs (**Figure 2.63**).

Figure 2.63: *Measuring fat below skin*

There are also digital devices which measure lean tissue mass and fat tissue mass (**Figure 2.64**). Tiny electrical currents are passed through body tissue to determine fat tissue from lean tissue (fat tissue doesn't conduct electricity very well).

Figure 2.64: *Digital balance which measures fat distribution*

Because fat is less dense than water, comparing the weight of an individual first in air then submerged in a water tank (**Figure 2.65**) enables measurements of body volume, density and body fat percentage. This is one of the most accurate ways of measuring body fat but it is very time-consuming. It requires the individual to be totally immersed in water so it is therefore not safe for young children or people with an existing medical issue.

TOP TIP

The best way to treat obesity is to eat a healthy, reduced-calorie diet and exercise regularly.

TOP TIP

Individuals are often advised to join a group to enhance their chances of persisting with a diet or an exercise programme.

Figure 2.65: *Water immersion technique to measure body fat percentage*

End of Unit Assessment

Key area 1 – The structure and function of reproductive organs and gametes and their role in fertilisation

1. The diagram below represents the appearance of an ovary when viewed under a microscope.

    (a) Name structure X. (1)

    (b) Identify using a line and the letter Y the most mature follicle shown on the diagram. (1)

    (c) Apart from forming and releasing ova, state **one** other important function carried out by the ovaries. (2)

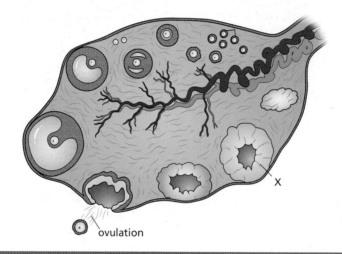

ovulation

Key area 2 – Hormonal control of reproduction

2. The diagram below illustrates some of the events involved in sperm production.

   (a) State the type of hormone which stimulates the pituitary and is released by the hypothalamus. (1)

   (b) Name the hormone secreted by the pituitary which promotes the secretion of testosterone. (1)

   (c) (i) Apart from the hormone named in (b), state the other hormone secreted by the pituitary which affects the process shown. (1)

   (ii) State the function of this hormone. (1)

   (d) Explain how this process is an example of negative feedback. (2)

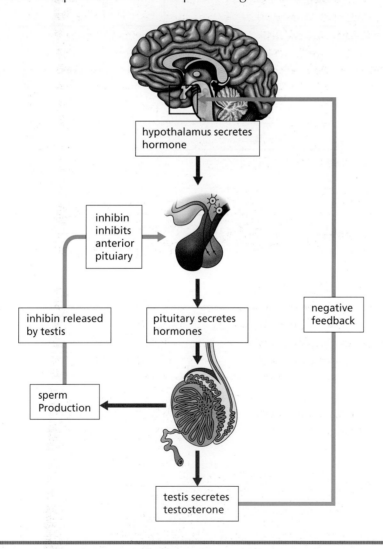

hypothalamus secretes hormone

inhibin inhibits anterior pituiary

inhibin released by testis

pituitary secretes hormones

negative feedback

sperm Production

testis secretes testosterone

Key area 3 – The biology of controlling fertility

3. (a) Decide if each of the following statements about contraception is **True** or **False** and tick (✔) the correct box.

   If the answer is **False**, write the correct word(s) in the **Correction** box to replace the word(s) underlined in the statement. (3)

Statement	True	False	Correction
<u>contraception</u> is the deliberate prevention of conception by natural or artificial means			
the mini-pill is an example of a <u>barrier</u> method of contraception			
vasectomy is usually <u>irreversible</u>			

   (b) The table below refers to semen samples in single ejaculations taken from four men.

Semen sample	A	B	C	D
number of sperm in single ejaculation (million/cm³)	56	64	50	54
volume of semen (cm³)	1.7	3.2	2.9	1.8

   (i) Identify which man has the highest number of sperm/cm³. (1)

   (ii) The World Health Organisation defines a normal sperm count as at least 20 million/cm³.

   Identify which individual does not have a normal sperm count. (1)

(c) The graph shows the blood testosterone levels, measured in ng/cm3, in young males aged between 12 and 17 years.

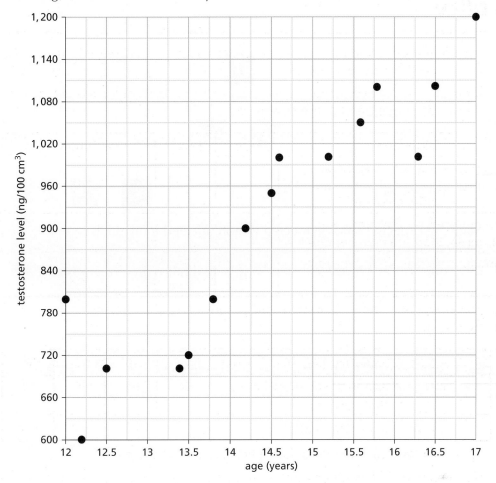

State the range of testosterone levels (ng/cm³) for these young males.   (1)

Key area 4 – Antenatal and postnatal screening

4. (a) Give **one** useful piece of information about a developing fetus which can be obtained from antenatal screening.   (1)

(b) Ultrasound imaging is a technique used to create an image of a developing baby.

State **one** use of an anomaly scan.   (1)

(c) State **one** advantage of chorionic villus sampling as a diagnostic tool.   (1)

5. The following family tree shows the inheritance of a sex-linked trait caused by a recessive allele (a).

(a) Using conventional symbols, identify the genotype of individual w.   (1)

(b) Explain why two of the sons in the F_3 (third) generation are affected but one is not.   (1)

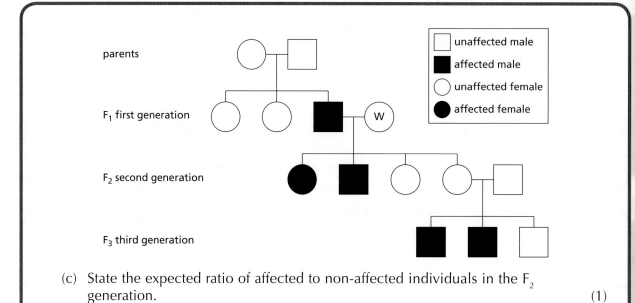

(c) State the expected ratio of affected to non-affected individuals in the F_2 generation. (1)

(d) Give **one** reason why the expected and actual ratios are not always the same. (1)

Key area 5 – The structure and function of arteries, capillaries and veins

6. The diagram below shows some aspects of the circulatory system.

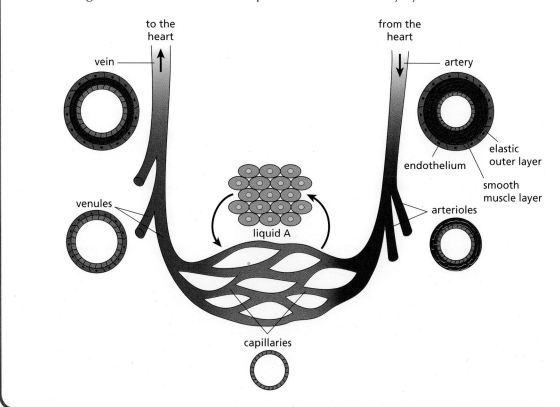

(a) Name the structures which are found in the outer layer of blood vessels and help give them the ability to expand and contract. (1)

(b) Name liquid A. (1)

(c) Explain how the structure of the endothelium of capillaries makes them efficient for the exchange of materials. (1)

(d) State **one** way in which the central lumen of an artery generally differs from that of a vein. (1)

(e) Give **one** structural way in which a lymphatic vessel differs from a capillary. (1)

Key area 6 – The structure and function of the heart

7. The following diagram shows some of the structures associated with the cardiac cycle.

(a) (i) Identify which of the two structures is responsible for originating the heartbeat. (1)

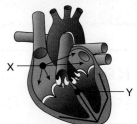

(ii) Name the structure you have identified. (1)

(iii) Name the part of the brain which regulates the rate of the heartbeat. (1)

(b) State in which phase of the heartbeat the left atrioventricular valve will be open. (1)

Key area 7 – Pathology of cardiovascular disease (CVD)

8. The diagram below shows a change which has taken place in an artery over a period of time in a patient whose family has a history of cardiovascular disease.

A

   (a) Name the fatty accumulation indicated by the letter A. (1)

   (b) Explain how the formation of this fatty accumulation can lead to an increase in blood pressure. (1)

Key area 8 – Blood glucose levels and obesity

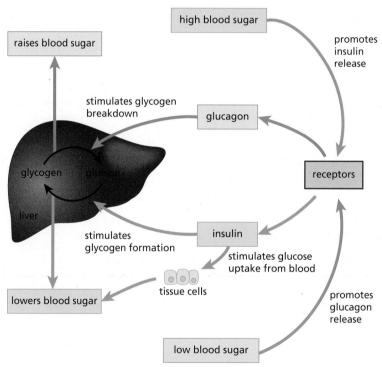

9. The diagram below shows how glucagon and insulin regulate blood glucose levels.

   (a) (i) State where the receptors shown on the diagram are located in the body. (1)

   (ii) Using the information in the diagram, explain how this illustrates a negative feedback mechanism. (2)

   (b) Obesity is linked to cardiovascular disease. One way of measuring obesity is using the body mass index (BMI).

   Explain how this can be used to identify individuals who are obese. (2)

(c) A group of slightly overweight men of different ages were tested for the prevalence of high blood pressure. The results are shown in the bar chart below.

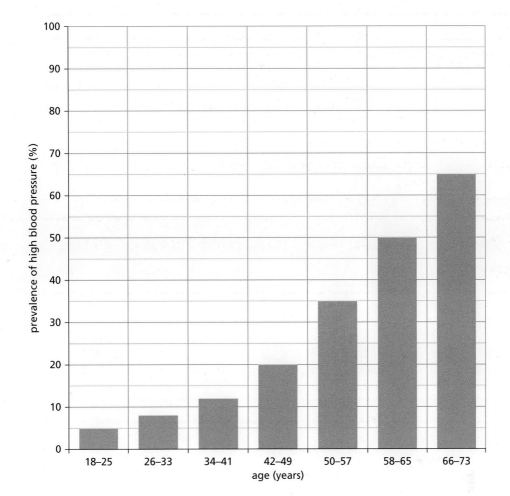

(i) Calculate the ratio of the percentage prevalences of men aged 45 years compared with men aged 62 years expressed as simple whole number ratio. (1)

(ii) Predict the likely prevalence for men aged 75 years. (1)

Divisions of the nervous system and parts of the brain

Central nervous system

The central nervous system (CNS), as shown in **Figure 3.1**, consists of the brain and the spinal cord and is responsible for receiving and sending information, and forming connections with other parts of the nervous system.

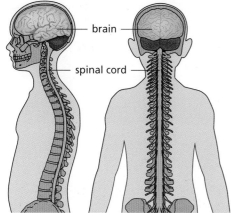

brain

spinal cord

Figure 3.1: *Central nervous system*

> ### TOP TIP
> An adult human brain is approximately 1.3 kg in mass and is the most delicate tissue in the body. A spinal cord is approximately 45 cm in males and 43 cm in females.

Peripheral nervous system

The **peripheral nervous system** (**PNS**) connects internal or external stimuli with the central nervous system, allowing the body to respond. Two systems make up the peripheral nervous system.

1. The **autonomic nervous system (ANS)**, which consists of the **sympathetic nervous system** and the **parasympathetic nervous system**. It controls and regulates actions which are involuntary. These include breathing, digestion, heartbeat and urinary functions.

2. The **somatic nervous system (SNS)**, which controls and regulates voluntary and reflex actions. Many of our unconscious reflexes are controlled by the SNS.

The two branches of the autonomic nervous system, sympathetic and parasympathetic, act antagonistically, that is they carry out opposing actions on the same structures, ensuring the optimum conditions for body functions.

> ### TOP TIP
> Antagonism is found in many different contexts. For example, the opposite actions of the triceps and biceps.

Cerebellum and medulla

The cerebellum and medulla (**Figure 3.2**) together form the **central core** of the brain. These two structures regulate vital life processes.

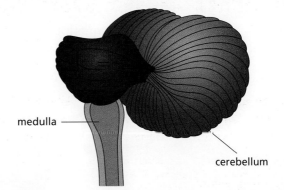

Figure 3.2: *Central core consisting of cerebellum and medulla*

Limbic system

Situated relatively deep in the brain is a group of structures called the **limbic system** (**Figure 3.3**).

This network regulates basic drives and emotions such as anger, fear, aggression, pain, hunger, sex and thirst. The limbic system is also linked to the formation of memories. It connects, in part, to the hypothalamus in the brain.

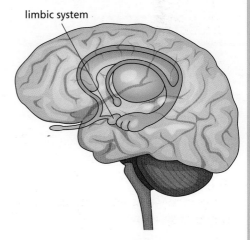

Figure 3.3: *The limbic system*

Cerebral cortex

The cerebrum is the largest part of the brain. Its outer layer, the **cerebral cortex** (**Figure 3.4**), receives sensory information, co-ordinates voluntary movement and makes decisions based on experience.

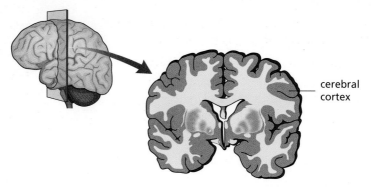

Figure 3.4: *The cerebral cortex*

Localisation of brain function

Particular parts of the brain, known as **association areas**, are linked to specific functions (**Figure 3.5**).

The frontal association area is concerned mainly with:

- higher-level problem solving
- reasoning
- intelligence
- the formation of core personality
- receiving sensory information from the cortex
- sending impulses to activate muscles associated with language production
- thinking
- behaviour.

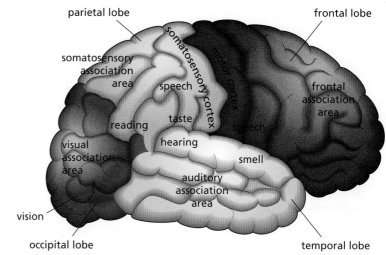

Figure 3.5: *Association areas*

The motor cortex controls voluntary movements involving muscles of the skeleton.

The sensory cortex receives impulses from sense organs such as the skin, muscles and other organs.

The visual association area receives impulses from the eyes and processes these into meaningful images.

Information from one side of the body is received and processed in the opposite half of the cerebrum.

Information from one side of the brain travels to the opposite side via a tract of nerve tissue called the **corpus callosum**, shown in **Figure 3.6**.

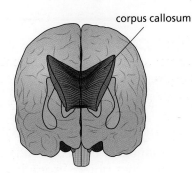

corpus callosum

Figure 3.6: *The corpus callosum connects both halves of the cerebrum*

Perception and memory

Perception

Perception is how the brain analyses and makes sense of incoming information. There are three areas of perception.

Segregation of objects

Segregation of objects is the process by which the brain distinguishes objects from their background or shape or from one another (**Figure 3.7**).

Figure 3.7: *Segregation of objects*

It is a complex process which depends on a number of learned cues being perceived and then integrated. Segregation of objects involves seeing boundaries between objects in our visual field. The cues involved could be separating the figure from the background to make an overall image, or between the sizes of objects in relation to each other so that, for example, an object in the distance will appear to be smaller than one in the forefront (even when both objects are the same size).

Distance perception

Distance perception relies on each eye seeing an object differently. The brain merges these two images to give a perception of distance, as to how near or far that object is. This is called **binocular disparity**. This is very useful when viewing objects which are familiar, when the experience of perceiving them is always the same, even when there are wide variations

Figure 3.8: *Perceptual constancy*

in the context or conditions of the observation. For example, as an object comes nearer, or the angle of viewing changes, or the level of illumination alters, the perceived size still remains the same. This is called **perceptual constancy** (**Figure 3.8**).

The perceptual set

Recognition relies on the ability of the brain to compare a perceived image or object or event and compare with its memory bank and recognise that this is not the first time this encounter has taken place. Shape is a primary feature in recognising an object (rather than its detailed structure) and assessing familiarity. A combination of past experience, context, and/or expectation impacts on recognition. This is called the **perceptual set** (**Figure 3.9**).

Figure 3.9: *Perceptual set*

> **TOP TIP**
>
> You can see how necessary two eyes are to judge distance by trying to catch a ball thrown from a distance when keeping one eye shut.

Memory

Most human behaviour is a function of memory, the ability to retain information about events, stimuli, experiences and ideas, even once the original stimuli are no longer in operation.

Memory involves three important and linked processes: storage, retention and **retrieval** of information (**Figure 3.10**).

Figure 3.10: *Brain progression*

Detection of environmental stimuli enters the sensory memory but is very short-lived. This information is transferred to the **short-term memory**, which is a temporary storage for information before it has been processed or interpreted. It has a limited capacity of around seven discrete items of information, which are held for a limited time. If the information is of no value, it is discarded but if it is potentially valuable, it is transferred to a long-term storage called the **long-term memory**, as shown in **Figure 3.11**.

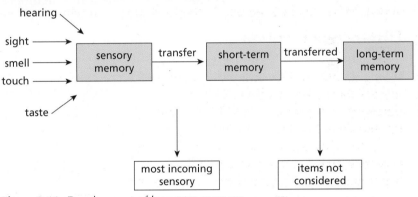

Figure 3.11: *Development of long-term memory*

When a number of items, such as a list of words, enter the short-term memory, those which arrive first and those which arrive last are better remembered than those items which arrive in between. This is known as the **serial position effect**, shown in **Figure 3.12**.

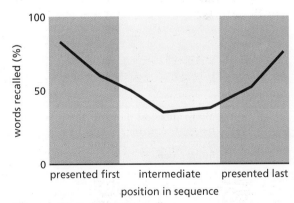

Figure 3.12: *Serial position effect*

One way of enhancing the short-term memory function is by repeatedly going over the items presented, extending the timespan of the information retention until the items become stored in the long-term memory. This is called **rehearsal** and is a common strategy used to retain information such as birthdays or telephone numbers (**Figure 3.13**).

TOP TIP

Recalling the most recent items depends on short-term memory while recalling the primary items depends on long-term memory.

Another commonly used technique for remembering lists of items is to group them in a meaningful way. For example, a candidate's examination number may consist of more than seven numbers but it can be stored as a single item like a birthday or a car registration number. This is called **chunking** (**Figure 3.14**).

The long-term memory has an unlimited capacity for the storage of information. Transferring information from short-term to long-term memory is enhanced by rehearsal, organisation and **elaboration**, or by adding more detail to a memory item making it easier to store by associating it with previously recorded material. The ability to recall anything in long-term memory is known as retrieval (**Figure 3.15**).

Figure 3.13: *Enhancing short-term memory function by rehearsal*

Incoming information from the sensory inputs must be encoded to change it into a form which can be stored and recalled later. For example, this could be using mental images, how something felt or sounded, or by forming linkages with information remembered already. Encoding using rehearsal is an example of a shallow type of encoding, while creating associative links is an example of a deeper type of encoding.

which is easier to memorise?
3,129,823,812
or
312-982-3812

Figure 3.14: *Enhancing short-term memory function by chunking*

Recalling information from the long-term memory is helped if the context of the encoding and retrieval are the same. For example, speaking to a friend might also be linked to the clothes he/she was wearing, the weather, time of day and so forth.

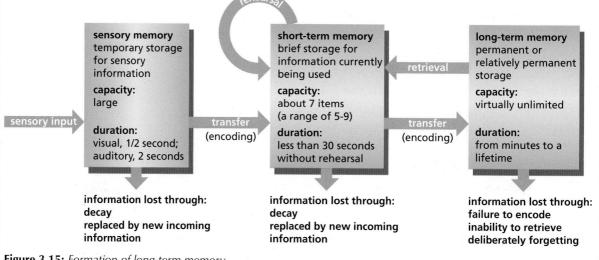

Figure 3.15: *Formation of long-term memory*

Different types of memory function are linked to different parts of the brain (**Figure 3.16**).

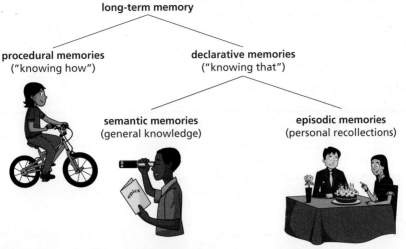

Figure 3.16: *Different types of memory function*

- the ability to remember personal experiences and facts is known as **episodic memory**, a form of memory in which information is tagged with where and when and how it was first perceived

- the ability to remember general information is known as **semantic memory**, a form of memory in which the meaning of information perceived is remembered

- memory related to motor skills or habits, such as riding a bicycle, is known as **procedural memory**

Figure 3.17: *Emotional memory*

- memories of positive or negative associations, such as love, hate, fear, sadness or joy, are known as **emotional memories** (**Figure 3.17**).

Spatial memory (**Figure 3.18**) is a form of memory which is linked to knowing where one is in space in relation to other objects.

Type of memory function	Location in brain
episodic	cerebral cortex
semantic	cerebral cortex
procedural	motor area of cerebral cortex
emotional	cerebral cortex and limbic system
spatial	limbic system

Figure 3.18: *Spatial memory*

Cells of the nervous system and neurotransmitters at synapses

Neurons

The nervous system is made up of neurons, as shown in **Figure 3.19**, which are capable of rapidly carrying information in the form of nerve impulses.

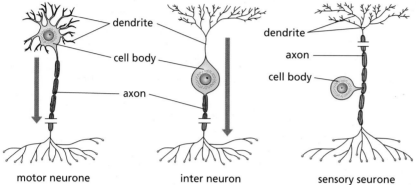

Figure 3.19: *Different types of neurons*

The three types of neuron are sensory, motor and inter. Each has:

- a **cell body** where the nucleus is located
- fibres called **axons** which carry nerve impulses away from the cell body
- fibres called **dendrites** which carry nerve impulses towards the cell body.

As shown in **Figure 3.20**, long neurons have a surrounding sheath made mainly of a fatty material called **myelin** which insulates the internal nerve fibre and allows the impulse to travel very quickly.

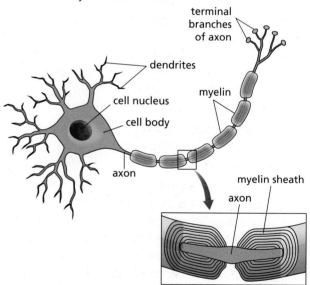

Figure 3.20: *Surrounding myelin sheath found in many neurons*

The laying down of myelin starts around the fourteenth week in the development of a fetus, but it is not complete at birth and continues into adolescence. This allows a child to crawl and walk within the first year (**Figure 3.21**).

Figure 3.21: *Development of walking*

Neurons have associated **glial cells**, which:

- maintain a homeostatic environment around the neurons
- form the myelin needed for the surrounding sheath
- provide mechanical support by holding the neurons in place
- supply nutrients and oxygen to neurons
- destroy **pathogens**
- remove dead neurons.

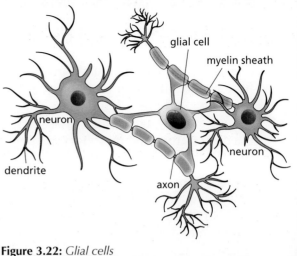

Figure 3.22: *Glial cells*

Neurotransmitters at synapses

The transmission of impulses from one nerve ending to another requires the presence of a chemical called a **neurotransmitter**. It is released at the end of a nerve fibre and passes across the synaptic cleft, shown in **Figure 3.23**, to the next fibre in line, causing it to fire, allowing the impulse to continue.

The neurotransmitter is released from small sacs called **vesicles** and diffuses towards receptors on the next fibres in line.

Once a neurotransmitter has carried out its function, any still remaining in the synaptic cleft are either degraded enzymatically to non-active products or are reabsorbed by the membrane at the end of the fibre along which the impulse was first initiated. One common neurotransmitter which is broken down enzymatically is **acetylcholine**.

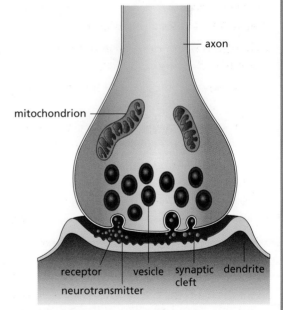

Figure 3.23: *Neurotransmitters travel across synaptic clefts*

The transmission of a nerve impulse across a synapse depends on the total secretion of neurotransmitter. If the stimulus is weak, not enough neurotransmitter will be secreted and the next fibre will not fire. Therefore a synapse acts as a filter preventing weak stimuli, such as a quiet sound or dim light, from generating a response. However, if enough weak stimuli are sent to a particular neuron, their individual inputs can collectively cause enough neurotransmitter to be secreted and the next fibre to fire. This is called **summation** (**Figure 3.24**).

A synapse also acts as a mechanism for a neuron to process a variety of incoming stimuli and to decide whether or not to secrete enough neurotransmitter to cause the next fibre to fire. This is because the plasma membrane of the next fibre has two different types of receptors, one promoting and one inhibiting the chance of an impulse being successful. These synapses are called **excitatory** and **inhibitory**, respectively (**Figure 3.25**).

Depending on the overall balance of the cumulative effect of all the excitatory and inhibitory inputs, the impulse either will or will not be transmitted.

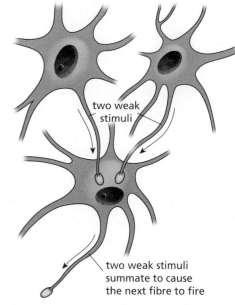

Figure 3.24: *Summation of nerve impulses*

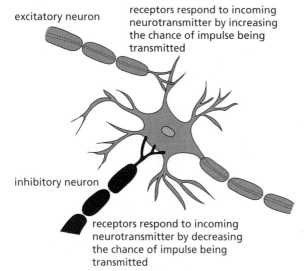

Figure 3.25: *Nerve impulse transmission can be modified by excitatory or inhibitory neuron action*

> ## TOP TIP
> Synapses are unidirectional, which means they ensure the impulse travels in only one direction.

> ## TOP TIP
> Over 100 neurotransmitters have been discovered.

Neural pathways

Neurons form synapses with other neurons in different combinations in the central nervous system. There are three pathways.

1. A **convergent neural pathway** where the stimuli from two or more neurons impact on one single neuron (**Figure 3.26**).

   The summation of many weak stimuli cause a nerve impulse to be generated in the single neuron on which many other neurons synapse. For example, a single motor neuron may need to receive impulses from different parts of the brain before it will fire.

2. A **divergent neural pathway** where the stimuli from one neuron can cause several other neurons to fire (**Figure 3.27**).

An impulse from one single neuron generates an impulse which causes two or more neurons to fire, possibly in different parts of the body. For example, an impulse from the hypothalamus can diverge into neurons affecting sweat gland secretion, skeletal muscles and changes in the diameter of blood vessels.

3. A **reverberating neural pathway** in which an incoming impulse travels along a chain of neurons (**Figure 3.28**).

   The travel of the impulse is maintained by impulses generated by the neurons in the chain, each one of which is linked with the previous cell by collateral synapses. These neurons are involved in the control of activities which are rhythmic, for example, breathing and the sleep–wake cycle.

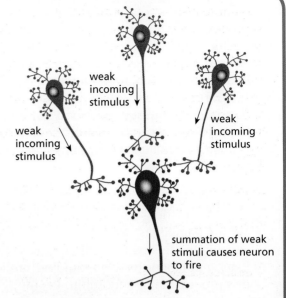

Figure 3.26: *Convergent pathway*

Previously it was thought that the brain's neural pathways were fixed but it is now known that the brain is in a state of continual change and reorganisation producing new connections, synapses and pathways. This enables humans to acquire new knowledge or learn new skills through experience. This property of the brain is called **plasticity**.

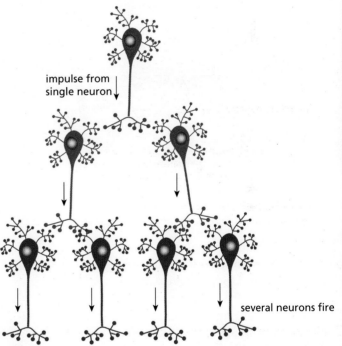

Figure 3.27: *Divergent pathway*

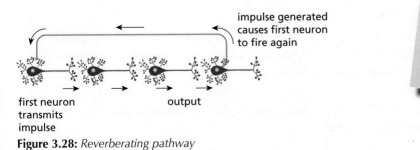

Figure 3.28: *Reverberating pathway*

TOP TIP

A single neuron can have thousands of other neurons acting on it.

Neurotransmitters, mood and behaviour

When the levels of neurotransmitters (**Figure 3.29 and 3.30**) are unbalanced, mood and behaviour can be affected. For example, loss of interest, low motivational drive, erratic behaviour and mood swings are all potentially influenced by neurotransmitter imbalance. Two neurotransmitters which influence mood and behaviour are **endorphin** and **dopamine**.

Endorphin

Endorphin functions in a similar way to naturally occurring painkillers, not only reducing pain but also enhancing the feeling of wellbeing. For example, the reduction of labour pains in childbirth relies on the body's production of endorphin. People with low levels of endorphin tend to feel more anxious and their pain thresholds are lower. Appetite control and the secretion of sex hormones are both linked to endorphin levels. Physical exercise produces a high which is linked to enhanced levels of endorphin.

Figure 3.29: *Neurotransmitter endorphin*

> **TOP TIP**
> The body produces about 20 different types of endorphin.

> **TOP TIP**
> Hibernation relies on endorphin to slow down the metabolism and heartbeat of animals.

Dopamine

Dopamine is an inhibitory neurotransmitter. Its presence will block nerve impulse transmission at a synapse. Dopamine is strongly linked to reward mechanisms in the brain, helping to raise motivation levels and promoting a feeling of wellbeing.

> **TOP TIP**
> Low levels of dopamine are observed in patients with uncontrollable muscle contractions, for example, Parkinson's disease.

Figure 3.30: *Neurotransmitter dopamine*

Agonistic and antagonistic actions

An imbalance of neurotransmitters can result in mental disorders, some of which can be treated using prescribed drugs like **agonists** and **antagonists** (**Figure 3.31**). They act on the receptors in the membranes of neurons, by either enhancing or inhibiting nerve impulse transmission.

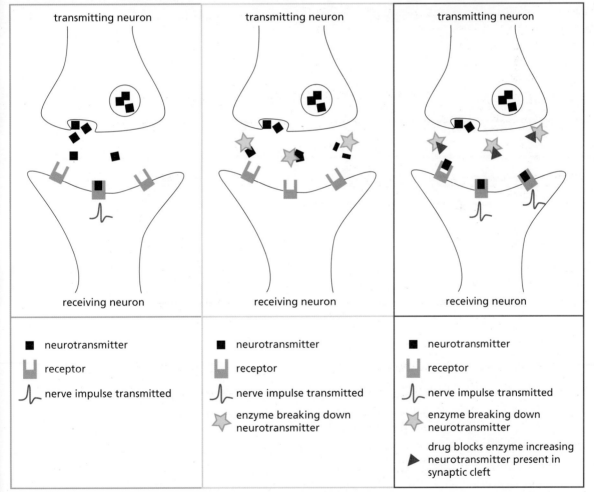

agonistic drug + receptor in membrane of neuron = agonist-receptor interaction → enhanced secretion of neurotransmitter and transmission of impulses

antagonistic drug + receptor in membrane of neuron = antagonist-receptor interaction → inhibited secretion of neurotransmitter and transmission of impulses

Figure 3.31: *Agonistic and antagonistic actions*

Prescribed drugs

Certain prescribed drugs can act as inhibitors of the normal enzyme function which breaks down a neurotransmitter.

transmitting neuron | transmitting neuron | transmitting neuron

receiving neuron | receiving neuron | receiving neuron

■ neurotransmitter

⊔ receptor

⎇ nerve impulse transmitted

■ neurotransmitter

⊔ receptor

⎇ nerve impulse transmitted

✦ enzyme breaking down neurotransmitter

■ neurotransmitter

⊔ receptor

⎇ nerve impulse transmitted

✦ enzyme breaking down neurotransmitter

◤ drug blocks enzyme increasing neurotransmitter present in synaptic cleft

Figure 3.32: *Action of drugs on enzymes involved in neurotransmitter function*

Other prescribed drugs slow down the reabsorption of the neurotransmitter (**Figure 3.32**) after an impulse has crossed the synaptic cleft (**Figure 3.33**).

Many drugs used to treat the imbalances of neurotransmitters are themselves very similar in their chemical structure to those neurotransmitters.

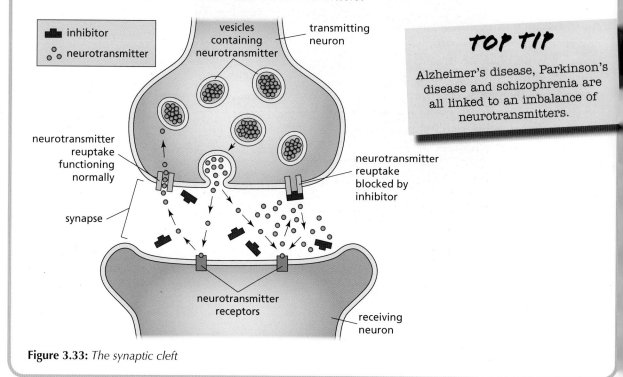

Figure 3.33: *The synaptic cleft*

TOP TIP

Alzheimer's disease, Parkinson's disease and schizophrenia are all linked to an imbalance of neurotransmitters.

Recreational drugs

Recreational drugs, as shown in **Figure 3.34**, are chemicals which mimic neurotransmitters and are taken for non-medical reasons such as:

- peer pressure
- experimentation with new experiences
- increased feelings of euphoria, relaxation and self-confidence
- relief of anxiety or stress
- performance enhancement.

By affecting the reward neural pathways in the brain these drugs can alter mood, perception, behaviour and thinking ability.

Some recreational drugs such as nicotine, alcohol and caffeine are legal.

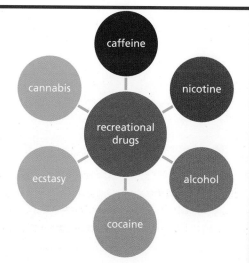

Figure 3.34: *Various chemicals used as recreational drugs*

Other recreational drugs such as ecstasy, cocaine and cannabis are illegal.

Repeated exposure to a drug can alter its effect in different ways, shown in **Figure 3.35**.

Figure 3.35: *Some effects of repeated drug exposure*

Sensitisation, shown in **Figure 3.36**, results from prolonged exposure to an antagonistic drug. There is an increase in the number and sensitivity of the binding neurotransmitter receptors formed. This may result in addiction and the experience of severe withdrawal symptoms if the drug is no longer taken.

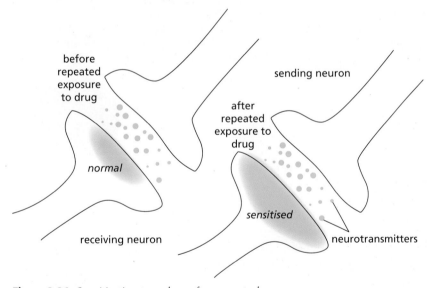

Figure 3.36: *Sensitisation to a drug after repeated exposure*

Desensitisation results from prolonged exposure to an agonistic drug. There is a decrease in the number and sensitivity of the binding neurotransmitter receptors formed. This may result in the same dose of the drug having less effect so that an increased dosage is required to achieve a similar high. **Tolerance** develops as this process continues.

Communication and social behaviour

Human beings are social animals which prefer to live in groups rather than isolation. Success in social grouping depends on communicating efficiently with other people using a variety of different media including speaking, writing and body language. This starts as a baby.

TOP TIP

The length of time an infant is dependent on its carer is the longest in the animal kingdom.

Infant attachment

A newborn baby depends totally on its carers as it develops into an infant. This results in a strong emotional bond called **infant attachment** (**Figure 3.37**), which develops through a variety of behaviours at various stages of development.

Studies suggest that infant attachment has a number of common characteristics which manifest themselves in three stages as the infant grows.

If the carer meets the needs of the infant then the attachment will be secure. If the carer ignores these needs (possibly expressed by crying) then eventually the infant will lose trust in the carer, leading to an attachment which is insecure. A study called 'The Strange Situation' was designed to observe infant attachment in children between the ages of one and two for periods of 20 minutes.

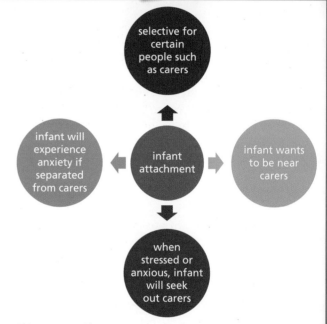

Figure 3.37: *Characteristics of infant attachment*

Stage	Age	Description
1	birth – 6 weeks	the baby does not fully recognise individual carers and reacts to them and objects in the environment in similar ways
		the baby starts to recognise the voice, face and scent of carers
2	6 weeks – 7 months	the baby starts to exhibit a clear preference for particular people, evidenced by smiling and eye contact
3	7 months onwards	development of attachments with individual carers
		demonstrates fear of strangers
		becomes anxious if separated from carer(s)

Here is a summary of the stages:

1. The carer and infant are both introduced into the experimental room and are left alone together.
2. The carer doesn't engage or become involved while the infant explores the unfamiliar surroundings.
3. A stranger now enters the room and talks to the carer.
4. The stranger approaches the infant as the carer leaves the room.
5. The carer returns and engages with the infant as the stranger leaves the room.
6. The carer leaves the infant alone.
7. The stranger returns.
8. The carer returns.

Four aspects of the infant's behaviour are observed:

1. To what extent the infant explores the unfamiliar surrounding (for example, by playing with toys).
2. The reactions of the infant when the carer leaves.
3. The reactions of the infant in the presence of the stranger when they are alone together.
4. How the infant reacts to the reunion with the carer.

Stage	Behaviour of infant		
carer and infant left alone together	explores the room and plays with the toys	explores the room but ignores the carer	stays with the carer and doesn't explore the room
the stranger enters	engages with the stranger	is at ease with the stranger	shows unease with the stranger
the carer leaves	becomes upset	shows no unease	shows intense distress
the carer returns	moves quickly to the carer	ignores the carer	behaves inconsistently, moving to the carer but then tries to escape contact
Categorisation of infant attachment displayed:	*secure*	*insecure avoidant*	*insecure resistant*

Based on these observations, infant behaviour is categorised as secure, **insecure avoidant** or **insecure resistant**. Of these, secure infant attachment indicates the ability to form stable future relationships.

The length of time infants need to develop means that they depend on their carers for a number of years. This affords opportunities for developing social skills which will enable an individual to modify their behaviour in order to meet with the demands of living in a community.

Effect of communication

Socialisation relies on the ability to communicate with other people (**Figure 3.38**).

Figure 3.38: *Communication is closely linked with social interaction*

While some communication is verbal, other communication is non-verbal (**Figure 3.39**). Verbal communication needs sounds and symbols.

Humans make extensive use of non-verbal signs and signals to convey emotions, messages and information. It is estimated that more than half of our information transfer is non-verbal.

A strategy which does not depend on spoken words can carry implicit messages, whether they are intentional or not. For example:

- reinforcing or changing what is said in words
- conveying emotional status
- making interpersonal relationships clear
- providing feedback to other people.

Figure 3.39: *Some of the many forms of non-verbal communication*

TOP TIP

What somebody is saying in words may not be what they are conveying by their tone of voice and/or facial expression.

Effect of experience

Activities such as riding a bike, or playing a sport which involves motor skills, need a lot of regular practice to develop those skills (**Figure 3.40**).

The long-term effect of practising increases the number of synapses in the brain. This sets up more and new neural pathways with increased myelination of the motor neurons leading to faster and stronger nerve impulses. Eventually the skill set required to play a musical instrument, or a particular sport, becomes so ingrained that conscious thought is no longer required to the same extent.

Figure 3.40: *Activities which involve sophisticated motor skills require regular practice*

Human behaviour is also learned by observing other people and copying their behaviour. This is called **imitation** (**Figure 3.41**). It is a common learning strategy adopted by children and adults.

Imitation leads to the development of cultural traditions. Information is transferred and passed on without genetic inheritance.

Several behaviours are learned by a process known as **trial and error**. This is characterised by a series of repeated and varied attempts to achieve a particular outcome, as shown in **Figure 3.42**.

Figure 3.41: *Imitation of behaviours shown by other people is a common form of learning*

child is out shopping with adult → child sees toy and asks to have this → adult refuses → child grabs toy and attempts to keep it → adult removes toy from child and returns it to the shelf → child throws a tantrum, screaming and attracting attention of public → in desperation adult buys toy for child

Figure 3.42: *A series of trials and errors may result in a desired outcome*

Trial and error:

- does not aim to discover why a particular outcome is achieved, simply that the strategy deployed works
- is highly specific to the particular outcome and doesn't necessarily work in other situations
- can waste energy because a large number of attempts to achieve a particular outcome may not succeed
- does not require in-depth knowledge of the situation
- is a good technique if multiple chances are given to solve a particular problem
- may be time-consuming.

Behaviour patterns can be reinforced, enhancing or inhibiting those behaviours, as shown in **Figure 3.43**.

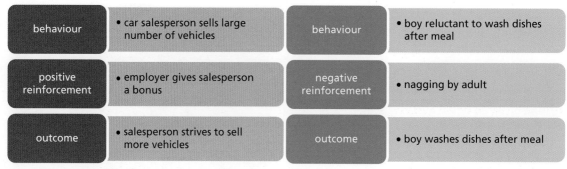

behaviour	• car salesperson sells large number of vehicles		behaviour	• boy reluctant to wash dishes after meal
positive reinforcement	• employer gives salesperson a bonus		negative reinforcement	• nagging by adult
outcome	• salesperson strives to sell more vehicles		outcome	• boy washes dishes after meal

Figure 3.43: *Positive and negative reinforcement of behaviour*

A complex behaviour pattern can be **shaped** by repeated use of reinforcements which become increasingly closer to the desired outcome (**Figure 3.44**).

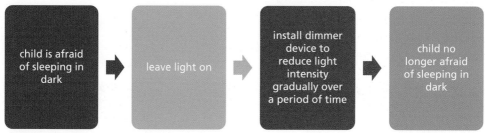

child is afraid of sleeping in dark ➤ leave light on ➤ install dimmer device to reduce light intensity gradually over a period of time ➤ child no longer afraid of sleeping in dark

Figure 3.44: *Shaping of behaviour*

If a behaviour is not reinforced it will eventually disappear. This is called **extinction**.

Occasionally the learned behaviour displayed in response to a particular stimulus is elicited by stimuli which are similar but not identical to the original. For example, an individual may have had a frightening experience with a loud barking dog making them afraid of all dogs. This is called **generalisation** (**Figure 3.45**).

As a child develops, the ability to distinguish between two or more similar stimuli improves so that they can make a different response to each one. This is called **discrimination** (**Figure 3.46**) and is a vital part of development which enables humans to react to similar stimuli in a different and appropriate way.

Figure 3.45: *Generalisation*

> **TOP TIP**
>
> Don't confuse negative reinforcement with punishment: punishment is the application of an unpleasant stimulus which aims to decrease undesired behaviour.

Granny Smith ▸ 4139

Figure 3.46: *Some people discriminate when choosing which apple to eat*

Effect of group behaviour and social influence

Humans have social identities as a result of operating in different types of groups and interacting with others (**Figure 3.47**).

Social groups share common characteristics and often feel a sense of unity.

There are four ways in which group behaviour can be influenced by social context.

Social facilitation

Social facilitation is linked to the perception of an individual's status in a social group which acts like an audience (**Figure 3.48**).

In a competitive context the performance of an individual is enhanced. For example, athletes perform better when running against others than on their own. Individual work efficiency rises when operating as part of a team.

Deindividuation

Deindividuation occurs when an individual's behaviour fits in with a social group. The attitudes and belief systems of the group become those of the individual. This is a classic strategy for changing the opinions and views of others. For example, most people would shun aggressive behaviour, but in a crowd that self-restraint may be reduced or disappear completely (**Figure 3.49**).

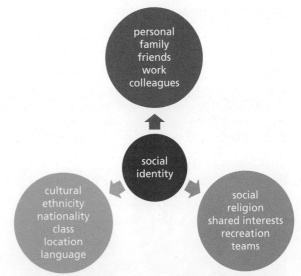

Figure 3.47: *Social identity involves interactions with different groups*

Figure 3.48: *Behaviour may be enhanced when performed within a group*

> ## TOP TIP
> Think of examples when people do things in a group they would never do on their own.

> ## TOP TIP
> Think of examples when deindividuation can have a beneficial effect on an individual's performance.

Figure 3.49: *People often behave differently when in a social group*

Internalisation

Internalisation is an individual's acceptance of a set of norms and values (established by others) through socialisation. The attitudes and belief systems of the group become those of the individual (**Figure 3.50**).

For example, a meat-eater continually in the company of vegetarians might be influenced to become a vegetarian.

TOP TIP

How do advertisers or politicians make use of internalisation?

Figure 3.50: *Internalisation*

Identification

Identification is linked to another person perceived as a role model. The individual wants to be like the role model and can become partially or completely transformed by copying their behaviour (**Figure 3.51**).

Advertisers exploit this by presenting what they are selling by using a famous personality.

Figure 3.51: *Identification*

End of Unit Assessment

Key area 1 – Divisions of the nervous system and parts of the brain

1. (a) The diagram below shows a side-view of some areas of the brain.

Complete the following table by identifying the regions of the brain labelled A and C and state **one** function of the *corpus callosum*. (3)

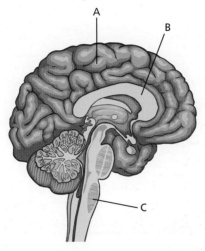

	Region of brain	Example of one function
A		co-ordinates voluntary movements
B	*corpus callosum*	
C		involuntary control of intercostal muscles and diaphragm

(b) The diagram below shows one way of dividing the central nervous system:

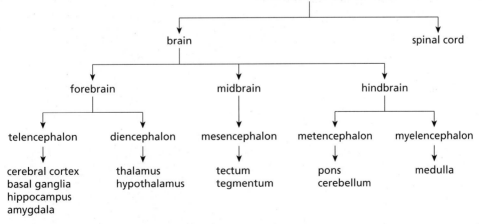

Using information from the diagram state:

(i) Where in the brain the tegmentum is located. (1)

(ii) **Two** facts about where the hippocampus is located in the brain. (2)

Key area 2 – Perception and memory

2. (a) The following statements refer to the sensory information needed for perception to occur:

   A   Distinguishing a figure from its background

   B   Binocular disparity

   C   Taking into account sizes and shapes of familiar objects

   Match each statement, using the appropriate letter, to these perceptual processes:

   Judging distance   ____   (1)

   Segregation of objects   ____   (1)

   Perceptual constancy   ____   (1)

   (b) After perception has taken place, the information may be passed to long-term memory via short-term memory.

   (i)   Describe **two** ways in which the transfer of information from short- to long-term memory can be brought about.   (2)

   (ii) Explain how chunking helps short-term memory function.   (1)

   (iii) Explain what is meant by a memory 'cue'.   (1)

Key area 3 – Cells of the nervous system and neurotransmitters at synapses

3. The diagram below shows a sensory neuron and its link to receptors in the skin:

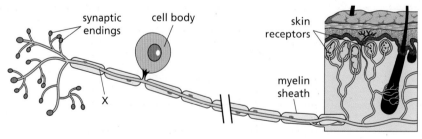

   (a) Name structure X.   (1)

   (b) State **one** way in which the myelin sheath helps the transmission of a nerve impulse.   (1)

   (c) At the synaptic endings, a neurotransmitter is released and comes into contact with the next neuron in line.

   (i) Explain how the neurotransmitter is stored in the synaptic endings.   (1)

   (ii) Some pain-killing drugs act by binding to the neurotransmitter. Predict what would happen to the perception of pain if one of these drugs was administered.   (1)

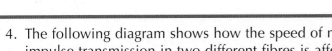
4. The following diagram shows how the speed of nerve impulse transmission in two different fibres is affected by the presence or absence of a myelin sheath:

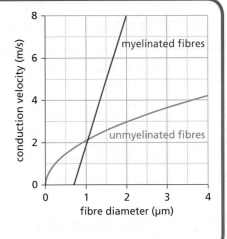

(a) Calculate the percentage difference in transmission between the two fibres when the diameter of both is 1.5 μm. (1)

(b) Some sensory neurons in the skin which are involved in temperature perception have a fibre diameter of about 1.6 μm. They do not need rapid transmission of their impulses.

State the type of fibre likely to be used by these neurons. (1)

Key area 4 – Communication and social behaviour

5. (a) State the term used to describe each of the following examples of social group influence on behaviour:

   (i) Cyclists tend to ride faster in the presence of their competitors than riding against time. (1)

   (ii) A student becomes vegetarian after sharing a flat with several others who are all vegetarian. (1)

(b) A person's facial expression and tone of voice can often convey their feelings.

State the term used to describe this form of information exchange. (1)

(c) The following table shows the distance a shot putter was able to throw in eight trials.

Trial	Distance thrown (m)
1	7.0
2	7.2
3	7.5
4	7.6
5	7.6
6	7.7
7	7.8
8	7.9

   (i) Predict how the distance thrown on a ninth trial would compare with the distance thrown on the eighth trial. (1)

   (ii) Give a reason for your prediction. (1)

Non-specific defences

Physical and chemical defences

Epithelial cells line the cavities and surfaces of blood vessels and organs throughout the body. They form a physical barrier and produce **secretions** against infection. Some examples of these are shown in **Figure 4.1**.

Epithelial cells are found in the lining of the lungs, the gastrointestinal tract, and the reproductive and urinary tracts. They constitute the exocrine and endocrine glands.

During an **inflammatory response** there is a release of **histamine** by **mast cells** causing **vasodilation** and increased capillary **permeability**. The increased blood flow and secretion of **cytokines** leads to an accumulation of **phagocytes** and the delivery of antimicrobial proteins and clotting elements to the site of infection. This is shown in **Figure 4.2**.

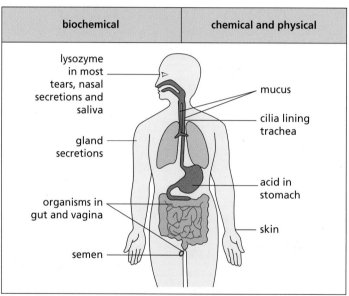

Figure 4.1: *Examples of secretions*

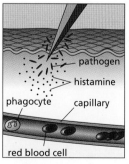

pathogen enters via wound

release of histamine by mast cells

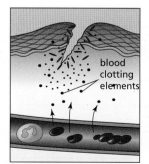

histamine causes vasodilation and increased capillary permeability

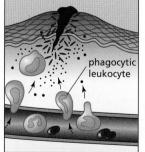

increased blood flow and secretion of cytokines

accumulation of phagocytes and the delivery of antimicrobial proteins and clotting elements

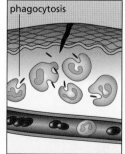

wound clotted

pathogen destroyed by phagocytosis

Figure 4.2: *Inflammatory response*

Phagocytes and apoptosis by natural killer cells

Phagocytes and **natural killer (NK) cells** release cytokines, shown in **Figure 4.3**, which stimulate the **specific immune response**.

Phagocytes recognise surface **antigen** molecules on pathogens and destroy them by **phagocytosis**. This process is summarised in **Figure 4.4**.

1. The phagocyte recognises the surface antigens on the pathogen.

2. The phagocyte ingests the pathogen and releases digestive enzymes from lysosomes.

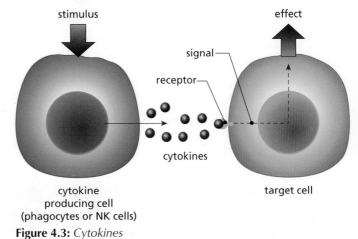

Figure 4.3: *Cytokines*

3. Enzymes destroy the pathogen and the contents of the phagocyte are expelled.

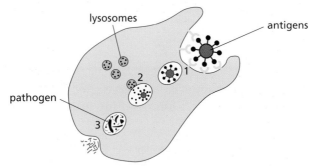

Figure 4.4: *Phagocytosis*

NK cells induce the viral-infected cells to produce self-destructive enzymes in **apoptosis**, a process of programmed cell death. This process is shown in **Figure 4.5**.

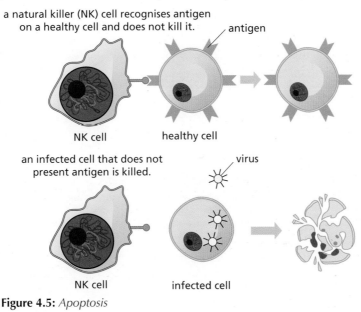

Figure 4.5: *Apoptosis*

Specific cellular defences

Immune surveillance

A range of white blood cells, some of which are shown in **Figure 4.6**, are continually circulating and monitoring the tissues. If tissues become damaged or are invaded, the cells release cytokines, increasing blood flow which results in white blood cells accumulating at the site of infection or tissue damage.

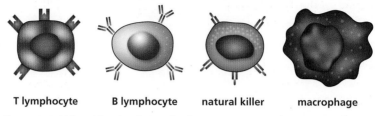

| T lymphocyte | B lymphocyte | natural killer | macrophage |

Figure 4.6: *White blood cells involved in Immune Surveillance*

Clonal selection theory

Lymphocytes have a single type of membrane receptor specific for one antigen. Antigen binding leads to repeated lymphocyte division resulting in a clonal population of lymphocytes, shown in **Figure 4.7**.

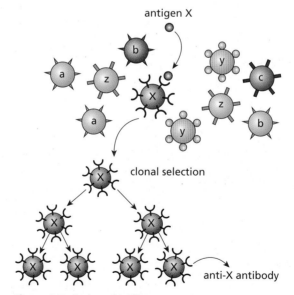

Figure 4.7: *Antigen binding*

T and B lymphocytes

Lymphocytes respond specifically to antigens on foreign cells, to cells infected by pathogens, and toxins released by pathogens.

T lymphocytes, sometimes called **T cells**, have specific surface proteins that allow them to distinguish between the surface molecules of the body's own cells, and cells with foreign molecules on their surface.

Failure in immune system regulation leads to **autoimmune disease**: T lymphocytes fail to recognise self-antigens and attack them by mistake, destroying healthy body tissue. This is shown in **Figure 4.8**.

normal immune response

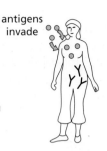
antigens invade
antibodies form

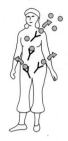
antibodies remove invading antigens

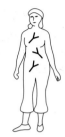
antibodies remain and protect

autoimmune disease

immune system forms antibodies to self-antigens

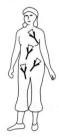
antibodies attack self-antigens

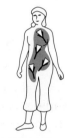
inflammation and tissue damage

Figure 4.8: *Autoimmune disease*

TOP TIP

In rheumatoid arthritis, cells in the joints produce cytokines that promote an immune response.

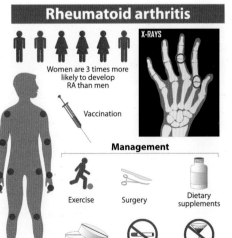

Rheumatoid arthritis

Women are 3 times more likely to develop RA than men

Vaccination

X-RAYS

80% of RA patients between the ages of 35-50

80%

70% of RA patients have wrist and hand problems

90% of RA patients have symptoms in the foot

Management

Exercise

Surgery

Dietary supplements

Antirheumatic drugs

Stop smoking

Limit alcohol

Risk

Heredity   Age   Lifestyle   Pollution

Complications

Heart attack   Stroke

Figure 4.9: *Overview of rheumatoid arthritis*

In type 1 diabetes, T cells attack insulin producing cells.

Figure 4.10: *A type 1 diabetic taking one of their regular insulin doses*

TOP TIP

In multiple sclerosis, T cells attack antigens on the myelin sheath of neurons.

Allergy is a hypersensitive B lymphocyte response to an antigen that is normally harmless. Examples include hayfever, asthma and food allergies.

Figure 4.11: *Hayfever*

TOP TIP

Hayfever is an allergic reaction where the B lymphocytes overreact to the antigens on pollen grains.

T lymphocytes

One group of T lymphocytes destroy infected cells by inducing apoptosis, a process shown in **Figure 4.12**. This is induced by T lymphocytes injecting **cytotoxins** into the cell to be destroyed. This causes a series of reactions to occur which eventually terminate the cell. The remains are ingested via phagocytosis.

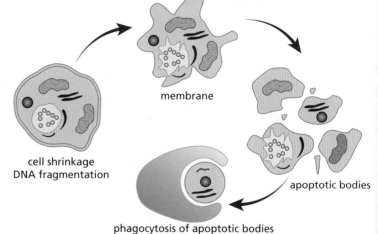

membrane

cell shrinkage
DNA fragmentation

apoptotic bodies

phagocytosis of apoptotic bodies

Figure 4.12: *Destruction of infected cells by inducing apoptosis*

Another group of T lymphocytes secrete cytokines that activate B lymphocytes and phagocytes, shown in **Figure 4.13**. These cells are called T helper cells due to their ability to help activate the other white blood cells.

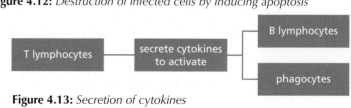

| T lymphocytes | secrete cytokines to activate | B lymphocytes |
| | | phagocytes |

Figure 4.13: *Secretion of cytokines*

When pathogens infect tissue, some phagocytes capture the pathogen and display fragments of its antigens on their surfaces, as shown in **Figure 4.14**. These antigen-presenting cells activate the production of a clone of T lymphocytes that move to the site of infection under the direction of cytokines.

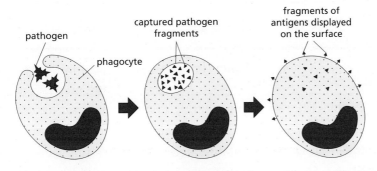

Figure 4.14: *Antigen-presenting cells*

B lymphocytes

Each B lymphocyte clone produces a specific antibody molecule that will recognise a specific antigen surface molecule on a pathogen or a toxin. **Antigen–antibody complexes** (shown in **Figure 4.15**) inactivate a pathogen or toxin or render it more susceptible to phagocytosis.

The antigen–antibody complex can stimulate a response which results in cell **lysis**. B lymphocytes activated by antigen-presenting cells and T lymphocytes produce a clone of B lymphocytes that secrete **antibodies** into the **lymph** and blood, making their way to the infected area.

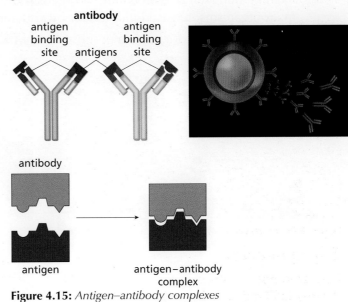

Figure 4.15: *Antigen–antibody complexes*

Immunological memory

Some T and B lymphocytes produced in response to antigens by **clonal selection** survive as **memory cells**. A **secondary exposure** to the same antigen gives rise to a new clone of lymphocytes producing a greater secondary immunological response. This is shown in **Figure 4.16**.

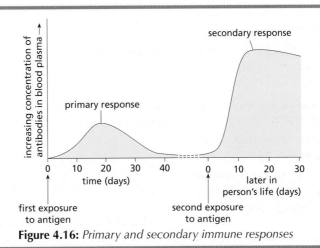

Figure 4.16: *Primary and secondary immune responses*

The transmission and control of infectious diseases

The transmission of infectious diseases

Infectious diseases are caused by pathogens. These can be transmitted, as shown in **Figure 4.17**, by:

- direct physical contact (for example, sharing contaminated syringe needles)
- water (for example, drinking water contaminated with microorganisms)
- food (for example, eating food contaminated with microorganisms)
- body fluids (for example, exchange of saliva or seminal fluids)
- inhaling (for example, breathing in the microorganisms, or droplets containing microorganisms, released into the air by coughing and sneezing)
- **vector** organisms (for example, mosquitos which spread malaria).

Figure 4.17: *Transmission of infectious diseases*

The transmission of infectious diseases is controlled, as shown in **Figure 4.18**, by:

- quarantine (the enforced isolation of the infected individual(s) to limit the spread of the infectious disease)

- antisepsis (the practice of using **antiseptics** to eliminate the microorganisms that cause disease)

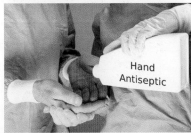

- individual responsibility (good personal hygiene and sexual health, and carefully storing and handling food)

- community responsibility (ensuring good quality water supply and waste disposal systems)

- vector control (the use of methods which limit or eradicate the organisms which transmit disease pathogens, such as mosquito nets).

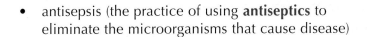

Figure 4.18: *Controls of infectious disease*

Epidemiology

Epidemiology is the study and analysis of the patterns, causes and effects of health and disease conditions in defined populations. Epidemiologists use the data collected to help prevent the spread and improve the treatment of diseases.

The spread of disease is shown in **Figure 4.19** and can be described as:

- sporadic (occasional occurrence)
- endemic (regular cases occurring in an area)
- epidemic (an unusually high number of cases in an area)
- pandemic (a global epidemic).

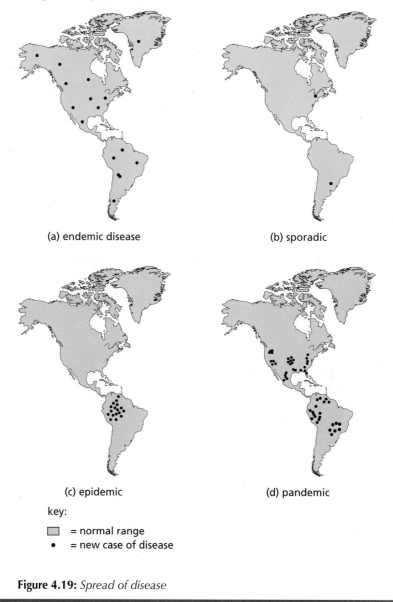

(a) endemic disease

(b) sporadic

(c) epidemic

(d) pandemic

key:

▢ = normal range

• = new case of disease

Figure 4.19: *Spread of disease*

The control of infectious diseases

Infectious diseases can be controlled using a number of methods:

- preventing transmission (avoiding all the possible ways of transmission)
- drug therapy (the use of antibiotics, antivirals and antimalarial medication)
- immunisation (**vaccinations**, which work by stimulating the immune system to become resistant to particular diseases, therefore protecting the body from subsequent attacks).

Figure 4.20: *Controlling disease*

Active immunisation and vaccination and the evasion of specific immune responses by pathogens

Active immunisation

Active immunity can be developed by vaccination with antigens from infectious pathogens, creating an **immunological memory**. Antigens from infectious pathogens, typically mixed with an **adjuvant** to enhance the immune response, include inactivated pathogen toxins, dead pathogens, parts of pathogens and weakened pathogens.

Vaccination

Vaccines, as shown in **Figure 4.21**, are subjected to clinical trials to establish their safety and **efficacy** before being licensed for use.

The design of **vaccine clinical trials** includes them being:

- randomised (the subjects are split into groups in a randomised way to eliminate bias)
- double-blind (neither the subjects, nor the researchers, know which group they are in, to eliminate bias)
- placebo-controlled (one group of subjects receives the vaccine while the second group receives a placebo to ensure valid comparisons).

It is important to have a large group of subjects participating in a trial to ensure statistical signicance.

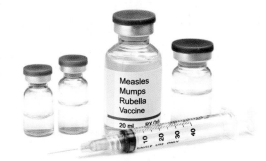

Figure 4.21: *MMR Vaccination*

The importance of herd immunity in infectious disease control

Herd immunity occurs when a large percentage of a population is immunised. Unimmunised individuals are protected as there is a lower probability that they will come into contact with infected individuals. The **herd immunity threshold** depends on the disease, the **efficacy** of the vaccine, and the contact **parameters** for the population. This is shown in **Figure 4.23**.

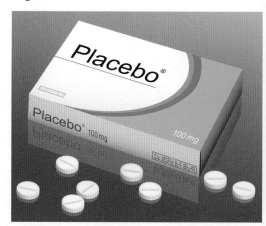

Figure 4.22: *Placebo*

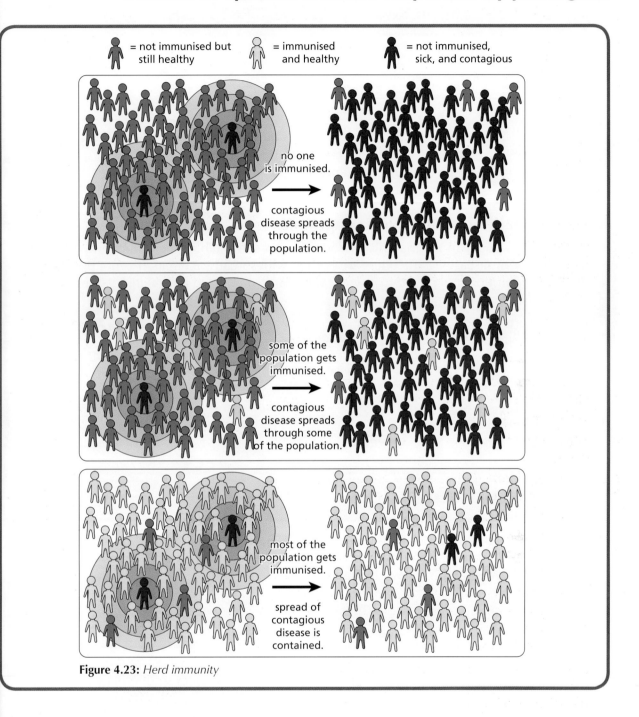

Figure 4.23: *Herd immunity*

Estimated herd immunity thresholds for vaccine-preventable diseases		
Disease	**Transmission**	**Herd immunity threshold**
diphtheria	saliva	85%
measles	airborne	92–94%
mumps	airborne droplet	75–86%
pertussis	airborne droplet	92–94%
polio	fecal-oral route	80–86%
rubella	airborne droplet	80–85%
smallpox	social contact	83–85%

Public health immunisation programmes

Public health policy in the majority of countries aims to establish herd immunity in regard to a number of diseases. Difficulties arise when widespread vaccination is not possible due to malnutrition and poverty, or when vaccines are rejected by a significant percentage of the population.

In many parts of the world, herd immunity can be achieved by using mass vaccination programmes and **combined vaccinations**.

> **TOP TIP**
>
> The measles, mumps and rubella (MMR) vaccine protects a child against three diseases in one injection.

> **TOP TIP**
>
> Several pathogens have evolved mechanisms that evade the specific immune system: this has consequences for vaccination strategies.

Antigenic variation

Some pathogens can change their antigens, enabling them to avoid the impact of immunological memory and destruction by the immune system. This is called **antigenic variation** and is shown in **Figure 4.24**.

> **TOP TIP**
>
> Antigenic variation occurs in the influenza virus: this is why it remains a public health problem and why those most at risk are vaccinated every year.

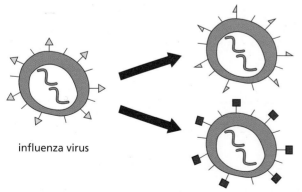

influenza virus

Figure 4.24: *Antigenic variation*

Antigenic variation occurs in diseases like malaria and **trypanosomiasis**. This is one of the reasons why they are still common in many parts of the world. Creating a vaccine for a continually changing pathogen is difficult.

Direct attack on the immune system

The absence or failure of some component of the immune system results in increased susceptibility to infection. For example, human immunodeficiency virus (HIV) is the major cause of acquired **immunodeficiency** in adults. HIV attacks lymphocytes and this is the main cause of acquired immune deficiency syndrome (AIDS). This is shown in **Figure 4.25**.

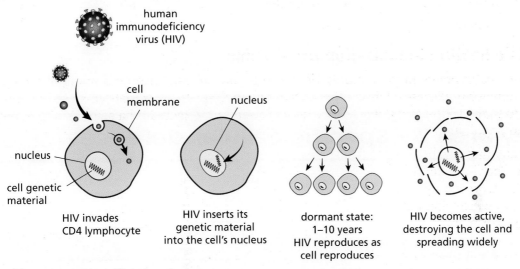

Figure 4.25: *HIV attack on lymphocytes*

Tuberculosis is a bacterial infection spread through inhaling tiny droplets from the coughs or sneezes of an infected person. It mainly affects the lungs. However, it can affect any part of the body, including the glands, bones and nervous system. It survives within phagocytes and avoids immune detection.

got it? ☐ ☐ ◯

End of Unit Assessment

Key area 1 – Non-specific defences

1. (a) (i) Name the cells which can form a physical barrier and produce secretions against infection. (1)

   (ii) During an inflammatory response, name the chemicals released by mast cells. (1)

   (iii) Describe **one** effect of the release of this chemical. (1)

   (b) Our bodies are defended by two types of white blood cell, phagocytes and natural killer (NK) cells. Choose **one** of these and describe how it protects the body against pathogens. (1)

Key area 2 – Specific cellular defences

2. (a) Draw lines to match each of the following terms with its correct description. (3)

Term	Description
T lymphocyte	Surface proteins which allow recognition of cells
B lymphocyte	Induces apoptosis
Antigen	Secretes antibodies

   (b) Describe what is meant by clonal selection. (1)

Key area 3 – The transmission and control of infectious diseases

3. Decide if each of the following statements about the transmission of infectious diseases is **True** or **False** and tick (✔) the correct box.

   If the answer is **False**, write the correct word(s) in the **Correction** box to replace the word <u>underlined</u> in the statement. (3)

Statement	True	False	Correction
infectious diseases are caused by <u>pathogens</u>			
<u>individual</u> responsibility includes having a good quality water supply			
transmission can be controlled by regulating <u>vectors</u>			

Key area 4 – Active immunisation and vaccination and the evasion of specific immune responses by pathogens

4. The table below shows the number of people infected with human immune deficiency virus (HIV) globally and the number with access to treatment.

Year	People living with HIV (millions)	People accessing treatment (millions)
2000	28.9	0.77
2005	31.8	2.2
2010	33.3	7.5
2011	33.9	9.1
2012	34.5	11
2013	35.2	13
2014	35.9	15
2015	36.6	17

(a) Select the year when the number of people living with HIV was less than 35 million but the people accessing treatment was more than 10 million. (1)

(b) Calculate the percentage increase in people accessing treatment between 2010 and 2014. (1)

(c) Using the data above, predict the number of people that will be living with HIV in 2016. (1)

(d) State **one** conclusion that can be drawn from the data. (1)

(e) Describe the effect of HIV on the immune system. (1)

5. (a) Describe the meaning of the term herd immunity. (1)

(b) State **one** of the difficulties with widespread vaccination. (1)

(c) Describe what is meant by the term antigenic variation. (1)

Glossary

accessory gland: group of cells attached to a larger gland which share a similar structure and function

acetyl coenzyme A: important intermediate metabolite linking glycolysis to the citric acid cycle

acetylcholine: chemical neurotransmitter found in many different locations

activation energy: the energy needed to break chemical bonds in the reactant chemicals

active immunity: the immunity which results from the production of antibodies by the immune system in response to the presence of an antigen

active site: area of the enzyme which binds to the substrate

adjuvant: a substance which enhances the body's immune response to an antigen

adrenal glands: endocrine glands which secrete several important hormones including adrenaline

affinity: the force by which atoms are held together in chemical compounds

agonistic drug: chemical which enhances the action of another chemical, such as a neurotransmitter

allergy: a hypersensitive B lymphocyte response to an antigen that is normally harmless

alpha-fetoprotein (AFP): substance produced by fetus which, if present in high levels in the blood of a pregnant woman, can help diagnose whether the fetus may have Down's syndrome

amniocentesis: technique used to diagnose potential congenital abnormalities by examining cells found in the amniotic fluid

amniotic fluid: watery liquid produced from the mother's plasma surrounding and giving protection to the developing fetus

amplification: creating many copies of a fragment of DNA

anabolic: synthesis of new molecules from basic building blocks using energy in the form of ATP

antagonism: having the opposite effect to another agent

antagonistic drug: chemical which inhibits the action of another chemical, such as a neurotransmitter

antenatal (prenatal) screening: use of diagnostic tests to look for any possible issues with a pregnancy

antibody: a protein produced by the body's immune system when it detects harmful substances, called antigens

anticodon: triplet of bases in tRNA that codes for a specific amino acid, and is complementary to a specific codon in mRNA

antigen: a molecule protein which provokes an immune response from the host body

antigen–antibody complex: a molecule formed from the binding of an antibody to an antigen

antigenic variation: the mechanism by which a pathogen alters its surface proteins in order to evade a host immune response

antiparallel: parallel, but running in opposite directions

antiseptics: antimicrobial substances that are applied to living tissue or skin to reduce the possibility of infection

apoptosis: a process of programmed cell death

array: a collection of microscopic DNA spots attached to a solid surface. For example, a probe

artificial insemination: introduction of sperm into the reproductive tract using an artificial means rather than sexual intercourse

association area: part of the brain dedicated to a particular function

atheroma: build up of fatty substances on the walls of arteries

ATP: adenosine triphosphate. High-energy molecule produced during cellular respiration

ATP synthase: an enzyme that catalyses the synthesis of ATP from ADP and inorganic phosphate

atrioventricular node: cluster of cells located in the wall of the right atrium, near the base, which passes the incoming stimulus from the sinoatrial node to the walls of the ventricles

atrioventricular valves: structures preventing the backflow of blood from the ventricles into the atria

autoimmune disease: the body's immune system attacks and destroys healthy body tissue by mistakenly failing to recognize self-antigens

autonomic nervous system (ANS): nervous system associated with unconscious control of internal body functions

autosome: chromosome other than a sex chromosome

axon: fibre in a neuron which carries nerve impulses away from cell body

binocular disparity: slight difference in the two images which are formed on the retina of each eye

bioinformatics: computer technology used to identify DNA sequences

biosynthetic processes: biological molecules join together to form larger, more complex substances, such as amino acids joining together to form proteins

blastocyst: ball of cells formed from dividing zygote which may implant into the wall of the uterus

body mass index (BMI): measurement involving height and body weight which can indicate levels of overweight

cancer cells: cells that divide relentlessly, forming solid tumours or flooding the blood with abnormal cells

cardiac cycle: regular contraction and relaxation of the heart chambers which make up one single beat

cardiac output (CO): volume of blood pumped by either the left or right ventricle per minute

catabolism: complex molecules are broken down into smaller subunits with the release of energy

cell body: structure in a neuron where the nucleus is located

cellular differentiation: the process where a cell changes from one cell type to another. Most commonly this is a less specialised type becoming a more specialised type, such as during cell growth

central core: consists of the cerebellum and medulla regulating the basic processes of life

central lumen: space within the blood vessels through which blood travels

cerebral cortex: outer layer of brain

cervical cap: artificial barrier method of contraception which fits over the cervix and prevents sperms reaching ova

cholesterol: insoluble lipid which forms part of an animal cell membrane

chorionic villus sampling: technique used to diagnose potential congenital abnormalities by examining cells from the placenta

chunking: organising distinct bits of information into a single whole, making them easier to recall

citrate: intermediate compound in the citric acid cycle

citric acid cycle: cyclical series of reactions operating under aerobic conditions in the mitochondrial matrix

clonal selection: antigen binding leads to repeated lymphocyte division resulting in a clonal population of lymphocytes

coding: sequence of DNA bases that enters transcription and translation, resulting in a finished protein

codon: triplet of bases in mRNA that codes for a specific amino acid which is carried by tRNA

coenzyme: a small, non-protein molecule which combines temporarily with an enzyme, allowing a reaction to proceed

combined vaccination: two or more vaccines which could be given individually are combined into one injection

competitive inhibitor: substance which binds reversibly to the active site of an enzyme, thus reducing the quantity of active enzyme available

complementary: two (or more) things together form a satisfactory or balanced whole

condom: artificial barrier method of contraception consisting of a thin rubber sheath placed over the erect penis preventing sperm from reaching ova

continuous fertility: ability of a male to produce viable sperms at a constant level during his reproductive life

Glossary

contraception: any method used to prevent fertilisation of an ovum by a sperm or the successful implantation of a zygote or birth itself

convergent neutral pathway: coming together of two or more neurons acting on one single neuron

corpus callosum: band of nerve tissue connecting the right and left hemispheres of the cerebrum

corpus luteum: structure formed from follicle capable of secreting progesterone

creatine phosphate: a reserve of high-energy phosphates in skeletal muscle and the brain

cyclical: ability of a female to produce viable ova within a limited few days each month

cytokines: substances which are secreted by certain cells of the immune system which have an effect on other cells

cytotoxin: a substance which has a toxic effect on cells

deep vein thrombosis (DVT): formation of a clot in vein in the leg

dehydrogenase enzymes: enzyme which catalyses the removal of hydrogen from a substrate

deindividuation: loss of an individual's sense of personal identity in a group context

deletion: a base deleted from the sequence

dendrite: fibre in a neuron which carries nerve impulses towards cell body

desensitisation: a decreased response to a drug due to the formation of fewer and less sensitive neurotransmitter receptors

diaphragm: artificial barrier method of contraception which is inserted into the vagina to prevent sperm reaching ova

diastole: phase of the cardiac cycle when the heart muscle relaxes

differentiate: when a cell becomes a specific, more specialised type of cell through gene expression

discrimination: ability to perceive differences between two or more stimuli

distance perception: allows brain to perceive an object as far or near because each eye sees an object slightly differently

divergent neural pathway: one single neuron generates an impulse which causes two or more subsequent neurons to fire

DNA polymerase: enzyme which adds complementary nucleotides to the deoxyribose (3′) end of a DNA strand

DNA probe: a fragment of DNA, variable in length, which is short and single-stranded and specific to a complementary sequence, allowing sequences to be labelled

dopamine: inhibitory neurotransmitter produced in the brain which blocks synaptic transmission and is strongly linked to reward mechanisms in the brain

drug testing: testing potential medications to treat disease

duplication: genes are copied and remain in the chromosome

efficacy: the ability to produce a desired or intended result

elaboration: any strategy for adding detail to a memory item to make it more likely to be stored

electrocardiogram: trace of the electrical activity of the atria and ventricles of the heart as they contract and relax in one heartbeat

electron transport chain: series of reactions which occur on the inner membrane of a mitochondrion during aerobic respiration and combine hydrogen and electrons with oxygen to form water

embolus: mobile blood clot

embryo: an unborn or unhatched offspring in the process of development

embryonic stem cells: stem cells removed from an embryo

emotional memory: form of memory linked to love, hate, fear, sadness, joy and similar feelings

endometrium: lining of the uterus

endorphin: morphine-like chemical produced by the brain which plays an important role in pain reduction

endothelium: layer of cells which lines the inside of a blood vessel

energy investment phase: stage where 2 ATP are invested into glycolysis

energy pay-off stage: stage where 4 ATP are produced during glycolysis

epidemiology: the study and analysis of the patterns, causes, and effects of health and disease conditions in defined populations

episodic memory: form of memory in which information is tagged with where and when and how it was first perceived

epithelial cells: line the cavities and surfaces of blood vessels and organs throughout the body

ethical issues: issues arising from a set of principles regarding moral values and appropriate conduct

excitatory synapse: junction which promotes the continuance of a nerve impulse

exon: coding sequence of DNA

expressing: the process by which information from a gene is used in the synthesis of a functional gene product

extinction: loss of a behaviour due to lack of reinforcement

extracellular: outside the cell

FAD: carrier molecule which accepts hydrogen ions

familial hypercholesteromia (FH): inherited form of hypercholesteromia within a family

fast twitch: muscle fibres which contract quicker, but easily fatigue

fatigue: a feeling of tiredness due to accumulation of lactate

feedback inhibition: a mechanism used by a cell in which an enzyme that catalyses the conversion of a substrate into a product becomes inhibited when that product accumulates

fermentation: breakdown of glucose in the absence of oxygen

fertile period: narrow window of around 3–5 days when a woman can conceive

fertility: ability of sperm to fertilize an ovum and create a viable zygote

fibrin: tough protein formed by the action of thrombin on fibrinogen

fibrinogen: soluble plasma protein made in the liver

fluorescent labelling: a fluorescent molecule that is attached chemically to aid in the labelling and detection of a biomolecule, such as a DNA sequence

follicle: small cellular sac which has secretory abilities

follicle-stimulating hormone (FSH): hormone secreted by the pituitary gland stimulating the growth of the follicles in the ovary in females. Promotes sperm production in males

follicular phase: stage in the menstrual cycle in which the follicles develop and their secretions start

frameshift: insertion or deletion of nucleotides which results in every subsequent codon to the right of the mutation in the base sequence being different and results in the synthesis of a different protein

frameshift mutations: insertion or deletion of nucleotides which result in every subsequent codon to the right of the mutation in the base sequence being different. Results in the synthesis of a different protein

gamete: a sex cell, either sperm or ovum, which possesses only half the diploid number of chromosomes

gene expression: the translation of a base sequence in a gene into an amino acid sequence, and finally a finished protein, through the processes of transcription and translation

generalisation: similar response to stimuli which are similar but not identical to the original stimulus

genes: the basic physical and functional unit of heredity

genomic sequencing: ordering the sequence of nucleotide bases in a genome

genotype: the alleles or 'forms of a gene' an organism possesses

germline cell: a cell which can give rise to a gamete

glial cells: found in the nervous system which support neurons as well as producing myelin sheaths

glycogen: main carbohydrate stored in animal liver made up of many glucose molecules

Glossary

glycolysis: initial series of reactions of cell respiration which take place in the cytoplasm, with or without the presence of oxygen

H ions: hydrogen ions

haploid gamete: a gamete possessing a single set of unpaired chromosomes

herd immunity threshold: the number of people who need to be immunised in order to achieve herd immunity

high density lipoprotein (HDL): lipoprotein which acts as a carrier for cholesterol

histamine: secreted by mast cells – causes vasodilation and increased capillary permeability

homeostasis: general term for the maintenance of body systems in a state of dynamic equilibrium through negative feedback

hypercholesterolaemia: high levels of cholesterol in the blood plasma

hypertension: blood pressure above normal for a particular age group and health status

hypothalamus: region of brain associated with regulating body temperature and sleep patterns

identification: mental process where an individual consciously or unconsciously takes on the attributes of another person or group

imitation: attempt by a person to copy the behaviour of others

immunodeficiency: a state in which the immune system's ability to fight infectious disease is compromised or entirely absent

immunological memory: the ability of the immune system to respond more rapidly and effectively to a pathogen that has been encountered previously

in vitro: an artificial environment outside a living organism. For example, a laboratory

in vitro fertilisation (IVF): causing fertilisation event to occur outside the body of the female in a laboratory

induced fit: describes the change in shape of the active site when a specific substrate fits

induced pluripotent stem cell: a specialised cell which is reprogrammed to an embryonic state and has the potential to become a different type of cell

infant attachment: binding relationship between an infant and carers

inflammatory response: the complex biological response of body tissues to harmful stimuli such as pathogens, damaged cells or irritants

inhibitory synapse: junction which inhibits the continuance of a nerve impulse

insecure avoidant attachment: form of attachment in which infants explored the strange room without any contact with the carer and showed no obvious anxiety when carer left

insecure resistant attachment: form of attachment in which infants showed great emotional distress when the carer left the strange room and reacted badly when carer returned

insertion: an additional base inserted into the sequence

internalisation: accepting beliefs, values, attitudes of others as one's own

interstitial cell-stimulating hormone (ICSH): in males promotes the secretion of testosterone by the testes

interstitial cells: cell found between seminiferous tubules which produces the male hormone testosterone

intracellular: inside the cell

intracytoplasmic sperm injection (ICSI): injection of a single sperm head into an ovum

intrauterine device (IUD): artificial barrier method of contraception which consists of a small plastic or copper structure inserted into the uterus

intron: non-coding sequence of DNA

karyotype: a way of representing the chromosomes found in a somatic cell nucleus classified according to their size and shape

lactate: end product of fermentation in human muscle cells

ligase: enzyme which joins fragments of DNA together on the lagging strand

limbic system: group of structures in the brain linked to emotional status and the formation of memories

lipoprotein: water-soluble protein combined with fat found in the plasma

long-term memory: storage function in the brain for memories which have been processed and deemed important to keep

low density lipoprotein (LDL): lipoprotein which acts as a carrier for cholesterol

luteal phase: stage in the menstrual cycle when the corpus luteum forms in the ovary and secretes progesterone promoting endometrial development

luteinising hormone: in females triggers ovulation and the development of the corpus luteum

lymph: a clear-to-white fluid consisting of white blood cells, mainly lymphocytes

lymphocyte: type of white blood cell. They attack bacteria in the blood

lysis: the disintegration of a cell by rupture of the cell wall or membrane

mast cell: a cell which releases histamine during inflammatory and allergic responses

matrix of the mitochondria: the inner section of the mitochondria

meiosis: cell division which produces gametes

memory cell: a long-lived lymphocyte capable of responding to a particular antigen on its reintroduction, long after the exposure that prompted its production

menstrual cycle: events surrounding release of an ovum followed by changes in the lining of the uterus, usually taking 28 days to complete

menstruation: loss of the lining of the uterus along with some blood

metabolism: the thousands of biochemical reactions that occur within a living cell

mini pill: artificial chemical method of contraception which uses only the synthetic version of progesterone

missense: substitution of nucleotide which results in a changed codon

mitosis: a process where a single cell divides into two identical daughter cells

morning after pill: artificial chemical method of contraception using high levels of synthetics versions of progesterone and oestrogen

multi-enzyme complex: the bringing together of all the enzymes involved in a series of reactions. The product of enzyme A is passed directly to enzyme B until it reaches the final product

multipotent cells: cells that can develop into more than one cell type, but are more limited than pluripotent cells

mutagenic agent: chemical or radiation which increases the frequency of mutation in the genome

mutation: a change in the genetic composition of a cell

myelin: white phospholipid material which is the main constituent of the sheath around many neurons

myocardial infarction: heart attack caused by an embolism blocking up the coronary circulation

myoglobin: an iron-binding and oxygen-binding protein found in the muscle tissue of vertebrates and almost all mammals

NAD: carrier molecule which accepts hydrogen ions

natural killer (NK) cell: a lymphocyte able to bind to tumour cells and virus-infected cells without the stimulation of antigens and induce the viral-infected cells to produce self-destructive enzymes in apoptosis

negative feedback control: type of corrective mechanism for restoring and maintaining the dynamic state of an organism's internal environment in which a departure from a set value for a variable is detected and a response made to reduce the intensity of the increasing stimulus

net gain: output minus the input

neurotransmitter: chemical which acts as a communication between one nerve fibre and another across the synaptic cleft

node: collection of one type of specialised cells enclosed in tissue of a different kind

non-coding: sequence of DNA bases that do not enter transcription and translation. No protein is synthesised

non-competitive inhibitor: substance which binds irreversibly to an area other than the active site of an enzyme, causing a change in the shape of the active site so that the normal substrate no longer fits

nonsense: substitution of nucleotide which results in a codon being changed to a stop codon

Glossary

nuclear transfer techniques: the introduction of the nucleus from a cell into an enucleated egg cell. The donor nucleus used for nuclear transfer may come from a differentiated body cell

nucleotides: building blocks of the backbone of DNA. Composed of a nitrogenous base, a five-carbon sugar (ribose or deoxyribose), and at least one phosphate group

oestrogen: hormone produced in ovaries which promotes the development of female secondary sexual characteristics and during the menstrual cycle helps develop a suitable environment for an embryo to develop

oral contraceptive pill: artificial chemical method of contraception using synthetic versions of the naturally occurring hormones progesterone and oestrogen which prevent the secretion of LSH and LH by the pituitary

oxaloacetate: intermediate compound which joins with acetyl coenzyme A to form citric acid

oxygen debt: a temporary oxygen shortage in the body tissues arising from exercise

parameter: a limit or boundary which defines the scope of a particular process or activity

parasympathetic nervous system: branch of autonomic nervous system which slows down processes in the body

pathogen: a bacterium, virus, or other microorganism that can cause disease

peptide bonds: chemical bonds which join amino acids together to form a polypeptide chain

perception: processes which gives meaning to sensory information

perceptual constancy: the experience of an object being seen as the same regardless of changes in the conditions of observation

perceptual set: combination of factors which leads the brain to perceive one thing rather than another

peripheral nervous system (PNS): all of the nervous system with the exception of the central nervous system

peripheral vascular disease (PVD): damaged blood vessels distant from the heart

permeability: ability of cells to allow substances to pass in and out

personalised medicine: treatment which is based upon an individual's own genome

phagocyte: a type of cell capable of engulfing and absorbing bacteria and other small cells and particles

phagocytosis: the ingestion of bacteria by phagocytes

pharmacogenetics: the study of inherited genetic differences in drug metabolic pathways which can affect individual responses to drugs, both in terms of therapeutic and adverse effects

phenotype: physical expression of genes in an organism's characteristics

phenylketonuria: inherited error of metabolism due to a lack of an enzyme which can cause brain damage in a developing baby

phosphofructokinase: enzyme involved in glycolysis. It can be inhibited by high concentrations of ATP and citrate

phosphorylation: addition of a phosphate group to a molecule

pituitary gland: hormone-secreting gland, located in the base of the brain, which produces hormones that control many functions of other endocrine glands

plasma: straw-coloured liquid part of blood in which cells are suspended

plasticity: ability of the brain to change and take over functions normally carried out by other parts of the body

pluripotent cells: cells that can develop into all of the cell types in the body

polymerase chain reaction (PCR): in vitro method of amplifying a sequence of DNA

polypeptide: a chain of many amino acids

postnatal screening: use of diagnostic checks after a baby is born to look for any abnormalities

post-translational modification: alterations to polypeptide chains following translation. For example, the addition of an iron atom in the blood protein haemoglobin

primer: short single strand of DNA bases required for replication to begin

procedural memory: form of memory linked to a set of motor skills and habits

progesterone: hormone produced in the ovaries which promotes development of the uterus wall and the implantation of the blastocyst as well as inhibiting further development of the follicle

prostaglandin: hormone-like substance produced by the seminal vesicles which stimulates contraction of the female tract

prostate gland: gland which surrounds the neck of the bladder in males and which secretes fluid components of semen

prothrombin: plasma protein made in the liver

puberty: time when a young person reaches sexual maturity and is capable of reproduction

pulmonary embolism: blockage of the pulmonary artery due to part of a thrombus breaking free

pyruvate: important molecule which is formed from glucose after glycolysis

recognition: an awareness that an image or object or happening has been encountered before

recreational drug: chemical taken for pleasure or enjoyment but not under medical supervision

regulations: a rule made and maintained by an authority

rehearsal: a way of retaining information in the short-term memory by repetition

respiratory substrate: a molecule from which energy can be liberated to produce ATP in a living cell

retrieval: process of recalling information from long-term memory

reverberating pathway: chain of neurons along which an impulse travels and is maintained by impulses generated by a neuron ahead

rhesus factor: antigen found on the surface of red blood cells

rhythm method: natural barrier method of contraception which does not use any chemicals or physical devices but relies on avoiding sexual intercourse during the fertile period

ribosome: site of protein synthesis. Composed of ribosomal protein and rRNA

RNA polymerase: enzyme which unwinds DNA during transcription. Also adds free nucleotides to a single strand of DNA to form a single strand of mRNA

RNA splicing: removal of introns and joining of exons to form a mature transcript

secondary exposure: second time that the pathogen infects

secondary tumour: occurs when cancer cells break away from the primary tumour and travel through the blood system to another part of the body

secretions: processes by which substances are produced and discharged from a cell, gland or organ for a particular function in the organism, or for excretion

segregation of objects: process by which the brain organises what is perceived into the background to make an image which is meaningful

semantic memory: form of memory in which the meaning of information perceived is remembered

semen: collective name for sperm and the associated fluids produced by accessory glands

semilunar valves: structures preventing the backflow of blood from the aorta or pulmonary artery into the ventricles

seminal vesicle: one of a pair of glands on either side of the bladder in males which secrete fluid to nourish sperms and promote contraction of the female reproductive tract

seminiferous tubules: threadlike tubules within the testes which produce sperm from the epithelial cells which line the cells

sensitisation: provoking of the immune system against a specific antigen

serial position effect: in a list of items presented to the short-term memory, those presented first and last are more likely to be recalled correctly than those in the middle

set point: value for some variable which, if departed from, sets in motion a corrective mechanism to reduce the change

shaping: gradual development of a complex behaviour by repeated use of reinforcement as the behaviour approximates to the desired outcome

short-term memory: storage function in the brain for memories which have not received much processing

Glossary

sinoatrial node: pacemaker of heart consisting of a cluster of cells located in the wall of the right atrium which controls the rate of heartbeat

slow twitch: muscle fibres which contract slower, but fatigue less likely

social facilitation: performance is enhanced by group context

somatic cell: any cell within an animal which is not a gamete

somatic nervous system (SNS): nervous system associated with voluntary and reflex actions

spatial memory: form of memory which is linked to knowing where one is in space in relation to other objects

specialised: differentiated cells with a specific function and unable to become any other kind of cell

specific immune response: specialised immunity for particular pathogens

sphygmomanometer: instrument for measuring blood pressure

splice-site: substitution of nucleotide at a splice site

starch: carbohydrate stored in plants made up of many glucose molecules

start codon: first triplet which codes for the start of a polypeptide chain formation. For example, AUG

statin: drug prescribed to help reduce high blood cholesterol levels

stem cells: unspecialised somatic cells in animals that can divide to make copies of themselves (self-renew) and/or differentiate into specialised cells

sterile: incapable of reproduction

stop codon: final triplet which codes for termination in polypeptide chain formation. For example, UAA

stroke volume: volume of blood pumped by one of the ventricles during a single contraction

substitution: a base replaced by another, with no other bases changing

substrate: a molecule upon which the enzyme acts

summation: additive effect of two or more weak stimuli to cause a nerve impulse to occur

super ovulation: release of more than one ovum as a result of hormone treatment

sympathetic nervous system: branch of autonomic nervous system which speeds up processes in the body

synapse: a junction between two nerve cells, consisting of a minute gap across which impulses pass by diffusion of a neurotransmitter

systematics: compares human genome sequence data and genomes of other species to provide information on evolutionary relationships and origins

systole: phase of the cardiac cycle when the heart muscle contracts

T cell: another name for a T lymphocyte

testosterone: male sex hormone manufactured by the interstitial cells which stimulates sperm production as well as the development of male sexual characteristics and prostate and seminal vesicle function

therapeutics: the branch of medicine concerned with the treatment of disease

thermal cycler: automated machine able to carry out repeated cycles of PCR by varying temperature

thrombin: enzyme which converts fibrinogen into fibrin to form a clot

thrombus: blood clot

tissue fluid: liquid formed when plasma is filtered through the capillary walls containing no cellular components or proteins

tolerance: when the effect of a drug becomes progressively diminished unless the dosage is increased

transcription: making a primary transcript of mRNA using a DNA sequence. Takes place in the nucleus of a cell

translation: production of a polypeptide chain informed by an mRNA sequence. Takes place in a ribosome

translocation: genes from one chromosome are added on to another chromosome

trial and error learning: learning by the elimination of responses which don't achieve the desired behaviour and the enhancing of those which do

trypanosomiasis: sleeping sickness, a vector-borne parasitic disease

tubal ligation: artificial barrier method of contraception in which the oviducts are cut and sealed

tumour: a swelling caused by an abnormal growth of tissue, either malignant or benign

ultrasound imaging: use of high frequency sounds to create images of internal structures

unspecialised somatic cells: undifferentiated cells capable of becoming any type of cell

vaccination: the administration of antigenic material (a vaccine) to stimulate an individual's immune system in order to develop adaptive immunity to a pathogen

vaccine clinical trial: a clinical trial that aims to establish the safety and efficacy of a vaccine prior to it being licensed

vasectomy: artificial barrier method of contraception which involves surgery to close and seal the sperm ducts preventing the release of sperm

vasoconstriction: narrowing of the arteries as a result of the contraction of the smooth muscles found in the walls, increasing blood flow

vasodilation: widening of the arteries as a result of the contraction of the smooth muscles found in the walls, reducing blood flow

vector organism: an organism that does not cause disease itself but which spreads infection by conveying pathogens from one host to another

vesicle: general term for any sac-like structure which contains fluid

weak hydrogen bonds: the bonds between the base pairs which hold both sides of a DNA molecule together

Answers to End of Unit Assessment Questions

End of Unit 1 Assessment

1. (a) Stem cell – unspecialised somatic cell that can divide to make copies of itself (self-renew) and/or differentiate into specialised cells (1)

   Tumour – a mass of abnormal cells (1)

   Germline cell – gamete, such as sperm or ovum (1)

   (b) The repair of damaged or diseased organs or tissues or a specific example of this (1)

2. (a) Hydrogen bond (1)

   (b) Y = phosphate,　　　Z = deoxyribose sugar (2)

   (c) Guanine (1)

   (d) Adenine and thymine (2)

   (e) Antiparallel (1)

3. True (1)

   False – thymine (1)

   False – ribose (1)

4. (a) X = exon, Y = intron (2)

   (b) RNA splicing (1)

   (c) Nucleus (1)

   (d) Cutting and combining polypeptide chains or by adding phosphate or carbohydrate groups to the protein (1)

5. Substitution – no (1)

   Insertion – yes (1)

   Deletion – yes (1)

6. (a) Amplification of DNA (1)

   (b) Separate strands (1)

   (c) Short sequences of DNA which start DNA replication (1)

   (d) Heat-tolerant DNA polymerase (1)

   (e) 1024 (1)

7. (a) Anabolic (1)

   (b) Competitive inhibition (1)

   (c) Decrease (1)

   (d) Feedback inhibition (1)

8. (a) Citric acid cycle (1)

   (b) Pyruvate (1)

   (c) Inhibitory effect / reduces / decreases rate (1)

   (d) Protein / amino acids / fats / fatty acids and glycerol (1)

9.

Feature	Type of skeletal muscle fibre	
	Slow twitch (type 1)	**Fast twitch (type 2)**
Activity most suitable for	Endurance activities	Sprinting, short bursts
Myoglobin present	Yes	No
Major storage fuels	Fats	Glycogen/creatine phosphate
Contraction speed	Slower	Faster
Contraction duration	Longer	Shorter

(1 for each correct line in table)

10. (a) As the concentration of glucose increases the rate of respiration also increases (1)

(b) 67% (1)

(c) 22 (1)

(d) Between 2% and 3% (1)

End of Unit 2 Assessment

TOP TIP
Make use of diagrams to help you learn the location of structures.

1. (a) Corpus luteum (1)

   (b) Identify follicle just before ovulation event (1)

   [The most mature follicle will be the one just before ovulation takes place]

   (c) They produce the hormones oestrogen (1) and progesterone (1)

2. (a) Releaser (1)

   (b) Interstitial cell-stimulating hormone (ICSH) (1)

   (c) (i) Follicle-stimulating hormone (FSH) (1)

   (ii) Promotion of sperm production (1)

   (d) As the levels of testosterone rise the pituitary secretes less ICSH (1) and FSH (1)

TOP TIP
Make use of flowcharts to help answer this type of question.

3. (a)

True	False	Correction
✔		
	✔	chemical
✔		

   (1 for each correct line in table)

   (b) (i) A (1)

   [Calculate the number of sperm/cm^3 for each man by dividing the number of sperm by the volume of semen.]

   (ii) C (1)

   [This male's sperm count/cm^3 is 17.2 which is below the World Health Organisation's definition of normal.]

   (c) 600–1200 ng/100 cm^3 (1)

   [A range means the lowest to the highest.]

4. (a) Age of fetus **or** risk of genetic disorder (1)

   (b) An anomaly scan is used to identify problems with the development of limbs and organs (1)

   (c) It can be carried out relatively early in pregnancy (1)

   [Note the advantages and disadvantages of each of the screening procedures which are available to a pregnant woman.]

5. (a) $X^A X^a$ (1)

   [Since she is unaffected, she must have at least one dominant allele. But she has a son who is affected and he must have picked up a defective allele on the X chromosome he inherited from his mother, who must therefore be heterozygous or a carrier.]

   (b) Mother must be heterozygous $X^A X^a$ and father is unaffected $X^A Y$ (1)

   (c) 1:1 (1)

   (d) The sample size is too small or the random nature of fertilisation (1)

   [Frequently the expected outcome and the actual outcome are different due to these variables.]

6. (a) Elastic fibres (1)

   (b) Tissue fluid (1)

   [This fluid is forced out of the capillaries by pressure filtration and bathes tissue cells.]

(c) Only one-cell thick (1)

[Remember this applies in other contexts, such as the wall of the alveolus in the lung.]

(d) The central lumen of an artery is much narrower than that of a vein (1)

(e) Lymphatic vessel is closed at one end but capillary is open / lymphatic vessel contains valves but capillary does not (1)

7. (a) (i) X (1)

   (ii) Sinoatrial node (SAN)/pacemaker (1)

   (iii) Medulla (1)

   (b) Left atrial systole (1)

   [As the left atrium contracts, the pressure forces the atrioventricular valve open.]

8. (a) Atheroma (1)

   (b) Artery becomes increasingly blocked / central lumen decreases / artery loses its elasticity / blood flow is restricted [any two of these four] (2)

   [Anything which slows down the flow of blood in a vessel will increase the pressure.]

9. (a) (i) Pancreas (1)

   (ii) As glucose levels rise above normal, more insulin is produced by the pancreas and this promotes the conversion of glucose to glycogen in the liver (2)

   or

   As glucose levels fall below normal, more glucagon is produced by the pancreas and this promotes the conversion of glycogen to glucose in the liver (2)

   (b) Indicates high body fat content in obese individual in relation to both height and weight and is calculated by dividing the body weight [kg] by the square of the height [m²] (2)

(c) (i) 2:5 (1)

   [Express the ratio of 25:50 as a simple whole number.]

   (ii) 80% (1)

   [Prediction assumes the same rate of increase as for previous years of 15%.]

End of Unit 3 Assessment

1. (a) Cerebral cortex (1)

   The corpus callosum connects both halves of the cerebrum/cerebral hemispheres (1)

   [The terms cerebrum and cerebral hemispheres are often used interchangeably.]

   Medulla (1)

   [Many autonomic centres are located here.]

   (b) (i) Midbrain (not mesencephalon) (1)

   (ii) Telencephalon **and** forebrain (1)

2. (a) B (1)

   A (1)

   C (1)

   (b) (i) Any two from:

   Rehearsal: repetition of information over and over again

   Organisation: adding structure to information/categorising information

   Elaboration: adding meaning to information/analysing the meaning of information (2)

   (ii) Involves grouping smaller pieces of information into single items / increases span of short-term memory (1)

   (iii) Stimulus which helps retrieve information from long-term memory / a link to the context in which a memory was created (1)

3. (a) Axon (1)

   (b) Speeds up the rate of transmission of impulse / insulates the nerve fibre (1)

   (c) (i) Vesicles (1)

   (ii) Pain perception would be diminished (1)

   [If the transmission of an impulse is blocked, the next neuron(s) will not fire so the perception of the pain is reduced.]

4. (a) Unmyelinated speed is 2.2 and myelinated speed is 4.4. The percentage is 100% (1)

   (b) Likely to be non-myelinated (1)

   [The graph shows that myelination at a diameter of 1.5 μm would cause the transmission to be very rapid.]

5. (a) (i) Social facilitation (1)

   (ii) Internalisation (1)

   (b) Non–verbal communication (1)

   (c) (i) The distance thrown would be greater (1)

   (ii) Practising improves motor skill/performance/motor memory develops (1)

End of Unit 4 Assessment

1. (a) (i) Epithelial cells (1)

    (ii) Histamine (1)

    (iii) Vasodilation / increased capillary permeability (1)

    (b) Phagocytes recognise surface antigen molecules on pathogens and destroy them by phagocytosis (1)

    or

    Natural killer (NK) cells induce the virally infected cells to produce self-destructive enzymes in apoptosis (1)

2. (a) T lymphocyte – induces apoptosis (1)

    B lymphocyte – secretes antibodies (1)

    Antigen – surface proteins which allow recognition of cells (1)

    (b) Lymphocytes have a single type of membrane receptor specific for one antigen (1)

    Antigen binding leads to repeated lymphocyte division resulting in a clonal population of lymphocytes (1)

3. True (1)

    False – community (1)

    True (1)

4. (a) 2012 (1)

    (b) 100% (1)

    (c) 37.3 million (1)

    (d) As the number of people living with HIV increases, the number of people accessing treatment increases (1)

    (e) HIV attacks lymphocytes which is the major cause of AIDS (1)

5. (a) Herd immunity occurs when a large percentage of a population is immunised. Non-immunised individuals are protected as there is a lower probability they will come into contact with infected individuals (1)

    (b) Malnutrition, poverty or vaccine rejected by a percentage of the population (1)

    (c) The mechanism by which a pathogen alters its surface proteins in order to evade a host immune response (1)

Index

Index

Index

Index

Index

Index